But He Says
He Loves Me

But He Says He Loves Me

Girls Speak Out on Dating Abuse

NICOLE B. SPEREKAS

Safer Society Press
PO BOX 340 • BRANDON • VT 05733

Copyright © 2002 by Nicole B. Sperekas. All rights reserved. No part of this publication may be reproduced, stored in a retrieval system, or transmitted in any form or by any means, electronic, mechanical, photocopying, recording or otherwise without the prior written permission of the copyright holder, except for brief quotations in critical reviews.

Restraining order forms reprinted with permission from
Bradford Publishing Co., 1743 Wazee St., Denver, CO 80202.

Editor: Euan Bear, Mountain Bear Services   Copyeditor: Linda Lotz
Interior design & composition: Jenna Dixon   Proofreader: Beth Richards

Printed in the United States of America by Malloy Lithographing, Inc.

∞ The paper used is this publication meets the minimum requirements of the American National Standard for Information Sciences—Permanence of Paper for Printed Library Materials, ANSI Z39.48-1984.

ISBN 1-884444-66-0 / $15.00 plus shipping and handling / order #WP079.
Order from:

Safer Society Press

PO Box 340, Brandon VT 05733.

To receive a catalog or to place a phone order with your Visa or MasterCard, please call 802-247-3132. For more information on The Safer Society Foundation and Press, please visit our web site: www.safersociety.org

---

Library of Congress Cataloging-in-Publication Data
Sperekas, Nicole B.
 But he says he loves me : girls speak out on dating abuse / Nicole B. Sperekas.
  p. cm.
 Summary: Explores how abuse works, provides ways to prepare yourself to end an unsafe dating relationship, and identifies support available to help yourself or a friend to recover from abuse and its effects.
 Includes bibliographical references.
 Contents: Dating safely—Danger signs—Emotional abuse—Verbal abuse—Physical abuse—Sexual abuse—Why abusers abuse—Effects of abuse on victims—Eleven manipulations abusers use—Eleven reasons why girls stay—Breaking through your denial—How to leave the relationship—Breaking up is hard to do—Next time—Lingering effects—Parents talk: how can we help?—How to heal after an abusive relationship—Healthy relationships—How to be a good friend—Facts to remember.
 ISBN 1-884444-66-0 (alk. paper)
 1. Dating violence—United States—Juvenile literature. [1. Dating violence. 2. Interpersonal relations.] I. Title.
HQ801.83 .S64 2002
362.88—dc21   2001059153

---

08 07 06 05 04 03 02 01   8 7 6 5 4 3 2 1   1st printing 2002

Contents

Acknowledgments	vii
Note to the Reader	viii
Cathy's Story	1

1. Dating Safely — 10
2. Danger Signs — 13
3. Emotional Abuse — 15
4. Verbal Abuse — 23
5. Physical Abuse — 29
6. Sexual Abuse — 37
7. Why Abusers Abuse — 43
8. Effects of Abuse on Victims — 50
9. Eleven Manipulations Abusers Use — 58
10. Eleven Reasons Why Girls Stay — 67
11. Breaking Through Your Denial — 76
12. How to Leave the Relationship — 85
13. Breaking Up Is Hard to Do — 92
14. Next Time — 99
15. Lingering Effects — 104
16. Parents Talk: How Can We Help? — 109
17. How to Heal After an Abusive Relationship — 114
18. Healthy Relationships — 118
19. How to Be a Good Friend — 121
20. Facts to Remember — 125

Dating Abuse Summary	130
Glossary	132

Appendices
- A How to Get Help — 137
- B Getting a Restraining Order — 140
- C Sexual Abuse — 144
- D Date Rape Drugs — 146
- E Are You Depressed? — 149
- F When a Girl is the Abuser — 151
- G Questions and Answers — 153
- H Further Reading — 158

About the Author — 160
About Safer Society Press — 161

Acknowledgments

I am grateful to many people who gave me support while I wrote this book. They read drafts, provided input, and encouraged me. At frustrating moments, Lois Barnes lent a sympathetic ear.

Special thanks go to Drs. Suzanne Kincaid and Hannah Evans. They reacted to the drafts and shared their expertise with me.

Ann Johnson, Mary Williams, Max Price, Francha Menhard, Karen Deurmyer, Sam Burke, Carol Davis, and Ann Boyd read and reread numerous drafts of this book.

My deep appreciation goes to a number of teenage girls who read the manuscript and responded to it.

Many thanks go to my editor, Euan Bear. In addition to her editing skills (which are considerable), she has an understanding of dating abuse that helped sharpen my thinking and my writing.

Finally, this book couldn't have been written without the trust and help of the many victims of dating abuse I have worked with over the years. I learned a lot from their courage and their determination to leave abusive relationships.

A Note to the Reader

The girls and boys in this book are composites of actual girls and boys I have spoken with and helped over the years. The experiences they had in abusive dating relationships are presented factually and accurately.

Cathy's Story

Hi, my name is Cathy. I'm seventeen and I just got out of a dating relationship that was abusive. This relationship went on for over two years before I was able to end it. It took me most of that time just to realize and admit to myself that my boyfriend was abusive. Here's a brief description of those two years.

I met Jerry in high school. I was a freshman and he was a junior. I hadn't dated very much in junior high and didn't have much confidence around boys. I felt envious of the other girls who were prettier and had lots of boys hanging around. They always had boyfriends.

When Jerry was friendly during and after class, I felt good. Maybe I wasn't such a wallflower after all! He walked with me to my locker and met me after school to talk. I loved the attention. He really listened and seemed to understand me. He even laughed at my jokes.

Soon, he asked me out to the movies. Finally I was able to say that I had a boyfriend and someone to go out with Saturday nights. My parents met him. They didn't like or dislike him at first. All they said was that he was quiet. I think he was a little shy around them.

About a month after we began to date, Jerry started telling me what to do. He didn't ask me if I wanted to go out. He always assumed that I'd go out with him. He stopped asking me what movie I wanted to see or even if I was in the mood for a movie. One Friday night I wasn't feeling too well and wanted to stay home in case I was coming down with something. Jerry said that I probably wasn't sick and he would really miss me if we didn't go out. So I went out.

Two months later, Jerry began to object if I spent time with my girlfriends on the weekends. He said that if I really loved <u>him</u> the way he loved <u>me</u>, I'd want to spend all my free time with him. I felt pressured to give up spending time with my friends. But I did love him, and he really made me feel special. I wanted to prove to him that I loved him, so I spent most of my free time with him.

Sometimes, when my parents set their foot down and said I couldn't spend every minute with Jerry, I resented it, but I also felt relieved. I could tell Jerry that my parents said no. This way, I didn't have to tell him that I wanted some space from him occasionally.

We had been dating for about six months when Jerry began pressuring me to have sex. He would say things like, "Everyone's doing it. Do you want to be the last virgin in the whole school?" Some of my girlfriends had been having sex with their boyfriends, and I was starting to feel like maybe there was something wrong with me.

For a while, I was able to put it off. But Jerry increased the pressure by saying that he loved me and if I really loved him I would do it with him. Since we had been doing everything but going all the way, what was the point of stopping now? I gave in. It made me feel pretty bad because I wasn't really into it, and I was still angry because he pressured me.

Pretty soon, he began to criticize me. I had gained maybe five pounds since we first met, and he'd say things like, "You could be the poster girl for Weight Watchers." He thought this was funny, but he hurt my feelings. He made other nasty comments about my weight or the way my hair looked or how I was dressed. I told him his comments hurt me, but he said that I took things too seriously and told me to "lighten up."

We argued a lot, and he'd blow up and storm out. Afterwards, we'd make up and things would be really nice, almost like when we started dating. The nice part would last only a few weeks. Then we'd start fighting again.

A year into the relationship, I found myself spending <u>all</u> my free time with him. I didn't have any friends because he wouldn't let me spend any time with them. My grades began going down because when we were together to study, he'd demand we do other things besides our homework. I had always prided myself on my grades, but now I was happy if I could pull Cs.

Then, about 18 months after we began dating, we got into an argument and he hit me. He said he was sorry and that it wouldn't happen again. I cried all night I was so upset. The next day, my cheek was red and my arm hurt and was black-and-blue where he had hit me. I used lots of makeup to cover up the marks on my face. It was early spring and still cool out, so I wore a pullover to cover the bruises on my arm.

A month later, we were arguing and he hit me again. This time, he said that he wouldn't have hit me except that he had had a bad day at work (he had a part-time job after school) and that I should have known not to argue with him. Again, I had to work hard to cover my bruises so nobody would know.

He was always very loving for a while after he'd hit me. I'd think that he really was sweet and loved me. I'd always think things were going to be wonderful again.

I guess I wasn't myself anymore, because my mother and sister were both asking me if something was wrong. I don't think my mother liked Jerry. I tried to tell her how special he made me feel. She just said I seemed depressed, didn't see any of my friends, and my schoolwork had slipped. She said she didn't know what to do.

About a week later, Jerry hit me again. I had a black eye and bruised cheekbone. I had to put on practically a whole bottle of makeup to cover the black-and-blue marks on my face.

A couple of former friends I thought had completely written me off asked me if I was okay. I denied there was anything wrong, but I think they suspected.

Jerry told me after he hit me that it was <u>my</u> fault, that I was negative and didn't know when to be quiet and that I should never bother him when he'd had a difficult day at school or at work.

The next day, Jerry called to arrange when to pick me up. He was real nice again. I told him I was doing something for my mother and I'd call him back later. I wasn't ready to see him again. I thought about how nice the relationship was at the beginning and what it was like now. I felt like I had been in a fog for almost two years.

Finally, I got it. I started to understand that Jerry was abusive. Almost a year earlier, we had had a class at school that covered abuse, but I never put two and two together. I'd been in denial all this time, unable to see that my own boyfriend was abusive! Part of me still couldn't believe that this was true and that I had let it go on for so long.

I sat down and listed all the signals I had ignored:

- Jerry became bossy, assuming I would spend all my time with him. He also began "calling the shots," making most of the decisions, like where we were going to hang out. Generally, I didn't like it, but he was my first real boyfriend, and I didn't want to lose him. I made myself think it was very grown up to let him take charge and make the decisions. I don't know why. Maybe it was all those old movies I watched — the man ordering from the menu for the woman.

- Jerry pressured me to have sex with him for several months before I finally agreed. I still wasn't emotionally ready to have sex, but I didn't want to deal with the verbal pressure he was putting on me. Unless I had sex with him, he would think I didn't love him. I now realize this was abusive.

- Jerry became verbally abusive, making nasty comments about my weight, how I looked, and the clothes I wore. Once he began to criticize me, he almost never said anything nice again — except when he was being Mr. Sweet after a fight.

- Jerry gradually cut me off from all my friends. I shouldn't say that he did it — I allowed myself to be cut off from my friends because I was trying to please Jerry by spending all my free time with him. He was possessive of me and got jealous if he ever saw me talking with other boys in the halls. Soon, my world was smaller and smaller, and I wasn't having much fun anymore — not with Jerry or with other friends. I had stopped going to all my after-school activities.

- Another sign of Jerry's emotional abuse was that he didn't even encourage me to do well at school. He kept me from doing my homework so I could spend time with him.

- I now realize that Jerry was manipulative. He played on my insecurities about having a boyfriend and was able to manipulate me into dropping my friends, ignoring my schoolwork, and dressing and doing my hair the way he liked. He also discounted my feelings.

- Besides all the emotional, verbal, and sexual abuse, Jerry finally abused me physically. He promised it wouldn't happen again, but it did. He made excuses for his behavior that I accepted. Then, he hit me again and told me that it was my fault!

Before our two-year anniversary, I made the decision to break up with Jerry. This was easier said than done.

When he called, he was so sweet, I forgot that I wanted to break up with him. I agreed to go out with him. He was very nice, so I let myself think that everything was going to be okay. A few days later, he yelled at me over nothing, and I began to have doubts again. I was afraid that Jerry would get angry and hit me again. In spite of my fears, I continued to go out with him for several more weeks.

I heard about a program for abusive teenage boys. It was a 36-week program. About 60 percent of the guys who went got better if they finished the program. Only a small percentage finished. I thought about suggesting this program to Jerry, except that I was afraid to.

One evening we were watching a movie and Jerry seemed very mellow and loving. After the movie I said something about needing to work on a project for school. Jerry screamed at me and said that I had destroyed the mood and that school must be more important to me than he was.

I tried to reassure him, but he kept yelling. I went to leave his house, but he blocked the door and told me that I wasn't going anywhere. I tried to talk with him, but he was completely out of control. Man, I didn't know what I was going to do!

He began hitting me, but there was a knock at the door. A neighbor asked if everything was okay. I don't know what would have happened if the neighbor hadn't come. I used this interruption to leave. I knew I was safe as long as the neighbor was standing there. I went home.

The next day, on the phone, I told Jerry I didn't want to see him anymore. I told him about the program for abusive teens. Do you know what he said? He told me that he hadn't loved me for ages but had kept seeing me because he didn't want to hurt my feelings. What a jerk.

Finally, I was determined to stay away from him. Believe it or not, there were moments, especially when I thought about how sweet he could be, that I thought about calling him. I was lonely. I was so out of touch with my friends that, at first, I had no one to talk to. I wondered if I was remembering right or if I was imagining his abusiveness. You don't know how close I came to calling him. I thought I was going crazy.

I worried that I would never have any boyfriends if I gave up Jerry. Everyone would know what happened, and no guy would be interested in me. I flip-flopped back and forth for the longest time, thinking of going back to him — if he'd take me back. This was the worst time in my life.

Breaking up with Jerry was the hardest thing I ever did. Even after not seeing him for months, I still had weak moments when I questioned my decision to leave him. I had to keep reminding myself that he was abusive and it wasn't my fault. I had to keep telling myself, "You don't deserve to be treated like this."

It took longer than I'd like to admit, but the struggle of breaking up with him is finally over. You know what I'm struggling with now? Not so much the loss of Jerry, though it still hurts. It's that I'm so angry with myself.

It was so important for me to have a boyfriend that I changed almost my whole personality and life to try to please him. I lied to my family. I made excuses for him. I even believed that any behavior he displayed toward me either wasn't abusive or was my fault.

How could I let myself be abused for so long? I now know that I was depressed for the last year of the relationship.

With the help of my parents, some of the friends I had dumped to be with Jerry, and a counselor, I'm beginning to feel a little better about myself. But the damage is so deep that I know it's going to take a long time to get over this.

This is the book I wish I had read — and listened to — during my relationship with Jerry. I know that my denial still would have kicked in, but maybe it wouldn't have taken me more than two years to end the relationship. There are good questions at the end of most of the chapters. They really make you think about what's going on and what to do about it. And unlike homework, there are no right or wrong answers.

Good luck in your own healing.

—Cathy

1 Dating Safely

As a teenager, dating is one of the most important events in your life. If you are a young teenager, it's mostly a way to have a good time with friends. If you're a little older, dating is often more serious and may eventually lead to marriage. Dating progresses from just having fun and a good time, to romance, to love, to intimacy, to commitment, and, for some, to marriage.

Because dating often leads to marriage, you need to consider the importance of dating. After your early teens, dating becomes a way to learn about yourself and the different personalities and traits you like in a boy or girl. It's also about learning communication skills and developing traits such as honesty, trust, and respect. Finally, over time, dating gives you the opportunity to be comfortable with intimacy and commitment.

Dating isn't always as much fun as you expected. It's not always easy. When you don't have experience, it can be hard to handle some of the emotions that develop in dating relationships. This is pretty normal, and most of us do better as we learn from experience.

A more serious problem involves dating abuse. It's more common than most people realize. According to surveys, violence takes place in about one out of four teen dating relationships. Dating abuse is about power and control. Dating abuse can happen to anyone, no matter what age, race, cultural group, gender, or family financial status.

But He Says He Loves Me: Girls Speak Out on Dating Abuse is for you if you have already experienced an abusive dating relationship or if you are in one now. If you think about your relationship, you may be able to list your date's abusive behaviors. You may have tried to break up with an abusive dating partner lots of times already. Or maybe you've successfully freed yourself from someone with problem behavior.

This book is for you even if you don't think you're in an abusive relationship right now. You may be one of the thousands of young adults in abusive relationships who don't even realize it. Your brain may know what's going on, but your heart denies it. Or you may need this information later, in a different relationship, to help you understand what's happening and how to get out. This book is for you if you have close friends who are in abusive dating relationships.

Maybe you're among the lucky ones who have never encountered an abusive relationship. But by learning the signs of dating abuse and how damaging dating abuse can be, you may be able to help a friend who feels trapped, and you're more likely to notice the signs in your relationships and have the strength and knowledge to get out.

While both boys and girls can be abusive in dating relationships, *But He Says He Loves Me* focuses on dating abuse when girls are the victims. If you're bisexual or gay, remember that people in same-sex dating relationships can be controlling and abusive, too. It can be even harder to get out, because the abuse might be blamed on the negative treatment gay people receive from society. And if you tell someone about the abuse, he or she might blame it on your being gay. If you are in a dating relationship with another young woman, this book can still help you. When you read it, change the pronouns for the person who is being abusive from "he" to "she" in your mind, and see whether the statement still fits what's going on.

But He Says He Loves Me gives you the facts we know about how abuse works so you can reject unsafe dating relationships. Dating should be fun and safe. When it's not, it's hard to be healthy and to grow emotionally and become a mature adult.

2 Danger Signs

Have you ever been in a dating relationship like this? (Remember that if your date is another girl or young woman, she may be doing these things, too.)

Your date:

- ☐ tells you what you can and cannot say.
- ☐ doesn't like it when you spend time with friends.
- ☐ makes you account for where you've been and who you've been with.
- ☐ calls you all the time.
- ☐ hangs out around your home, school, or job and gives you some flimsy "reason."
- ☐ makes you feel tense and afraid, like you're walking on tiptoe all the time.
- ☐ wants you to spend all your free time with him.

- ☐ plays mind games to trap or trick you into saying or doing what he wants.
- ☐ makes all the decisions.
- ☐ puts you down verbally — calls you names or ridicules you or is highly critical of you for no apparent reason.
- ☐ discounts your feelings, your words, or your behavior.
- ☐ blames you for anything that goes wrong in the relationship.
- ☐ threatens you verbally.
- ☐ makes it hard for you to leave the relationship — won't let go.
- ☐ becomes angry over small things.
- ☐ behaves in ways that feel scary, so you begin to change what you say and how you act to calm him down or please him.
- ☐ does drugs and/or drinks alcohol a lot, or drives when drunk or drugged and expects you to ride with him.
- ☐ pressures you to do things that are against the law.
- ☐ pressures you sexually or has bullied or forced you into having sex when you didn't want to (rape).
- ☐ shoves, pushes, kicks, slaps, or hits you.
- ☐ uses various kinds of power to control you.

If you checked off two or more of these statements, it is likely that you are in an abusive dating situation.

3 Emotional Abuse

I don't completely understand how it happened. Little by little, he expected me to devote all my free time to him. After a while, I lost all my friends. He wouldn't let me see them. If I just looked at a boy in the halls for more than two seconds, he'd get jealous and angry.

— Juanita, 15

Last year Juanita was a freshman in high school. She was in a special school-to-career program with regular high school classes in the mornings. In the afternoons, she attended a vocational school with a restaurant management and cooking school and other career training courses. Juanita was learning to be a chef. When she finished high school, she would have the qualifications and experience to be hired as a chef at a nice restaurant.

She loved her cooking classes. It was a lot of work, but it was fun. Every week she learned new recipes and made them in class. For tests, she had to memorize recipes, be able to define cooking terms, and show that she had learned certain techniques. Her life was going pretty well. Then she met Marco.

Looking back on her relationship with Marco, Juanita could see how the *emotional abuse* started very subtly. Later, it became more obvious.

Isolation

A month into the relationship, Marco didn't want Juanita to be socializing with anyone else. She used to go over to friends' houses after school to try new recipes. But Marco didn't like her hanging out with any of the kids in her cooking class.

> *When I tried to include other kids when we went on dates, he told me he only wanted to be with me. Eventually, I felt like a prisoner. But prisoners have more freedom than I did because they can at least talk to other prisoners.*

Isolation is one way to control another person and make her dependent on the controller. When your dating partner or boyfriend is into this kind of control, you get cut off from your friends and family.

Control

Most abusive people are control freaks.

Marco just had to be in complete charge of the relationship. At first I didn't see it that way. It seemed like he just cared very much and wanted to be <u>involved</u> in every decision. Soon, he <u>made</u> all the decisions — where we went, how long we stayed, when we left, what malls we went to, what we ate. He didn't even ask me what I wanted.

Jealousy

If your date gets upset if you speak with or want to spend time with other friends or accuses you of flirting or teasing other boys, that's jealousy.

If Marco saw me just say hi to another boy, he was jealous. He would have a snit fit. Ay! I couldn't calm him down.

Extremely jealous people may order you not to speak with or see old friends because it feels threatening to them.

I'd known Rico Zombola since second grade. Rico's like my brother. But Marco didn't believe we were just good friends. He accused me of having sex with Rico. He told me that if I was friendly to Rico again, it was over between us.

Jealousy is a form of control. It controls who you can or can't socialize with. Some girls ignore their boyfriends' jealousy. They think it's cute or that it's a sign of how much their boyfriends really love them.

At first, Marco's jealousy was cool. I thought it showed he really cared, but I was wrong. His jealousy was a kind of power trip. He just covered up his need to control everything by telling me that he loved me. What's weird is that Marco never had a clue that he was doing this from his own need to control me. If I had ever tried to tell him that his jealousy was about controlling me, he would have said I was crazy.

Possessiveness

If your dating partner treats you like property that belongs to him, this is possessiveness.

Marco made me feel like he owned me. Everything I did was up to his approval. He commented on how much time we spent together, what we did together, what clothes he wanted me to wear, how much makeup I wore, and what length and style I wore my hair. One time I cut my hair about an inch and he told me never to do that again without asking him first.

Soon, he wanted to know my every thought and everything I did during the day. Talk about mind games. I lost all my privacy.

Stalking

You know your date is stalking you when he pops up at unexpected times and places. He looks like he's trying not to let you see him, but he can see you. He seems to be spying on you, checking up on what you're doing, where you are, and who you're with.

It was the weirdest thing. Everywhere I turned, Marco popped up. I could be at cooking school and would see his car passing by. I would visit a friend down the street when Marco should have been at work, and sure enough, Marco's car was parked about a half block away. These things happened a lot. He would pop up out of nowhere. Whenever I confronted him, he told me it was just something that happened or that he got off work early. Then, one day I was in the halls at cooking school and Marco was there. He told me he had signed up for a welding class. He'd never mentioned an interest in welding to me before.

When caught at this cat-and-mouse game, people often try to deny that they were stalking. It was a "coincidence," they say. Some stalkers may more or less admit that they were there, but they tell you that they are just keeping an eye on you to make sure you are safe.

One time Marco told me he was worried about me because there had been a robbery a couple of miles away a few weeks before. I don't think there even was a robbery. He was checking up on me, making sure I was where I said I was going to be. It was another way for him to control me.

A more serious form of stalking is when your dating partner or boyfriend makes sure you see him following you. He wants you to know he's around. He wants you to feel anxious, afraid, or threatened by his presence. This is a more serious abuse of power, intimidation, and control. These stalkers can be dangerous. This kind of stalking may be a first step in a plan to hurt or possibly kill you. (Remember, animals in the wild stalk their prey prior to eating them.) If you are in a relationship with someone who is stalking you this way, you need to **get help now!** Tell your parents, your friends, a therapist, a teacher, or a counselor. Call a domestic abuse hot line for advice, then follow it. Call the police and get a restraining order or a protection order if you can (there's more on that later in this book).

Sometimes a dating partner continues to check up on you or to force unwanted contact by using a computer. This activity is called cyberstalking, and it may happen by e-mail, through chat rooms, or by instant messaging systems. If your dating partner is cyberstalking you, the best response is no response beyond "Stop contacting me." If your request for no contact is ignored, get in touch with www.cyberangels.com or www.haltabuse.com.

Manipulation and Coercion

Manipulation and coercion are also forms of control. They can be very subtle or very obvious. Manipulation is a technique to get you to do something you might not otherwise do. It plays on your emotions and feelings. Coercion usually involves the threat or use of power or force.

Juanita eventually figured out how Marco had manipulated her into doing his homework.

Marco always told me how smart I was. Then he asked me to do his homework for him because I was smart.

Does your date tell you that he plans to spend all his spare time with you?

He said he didn't want to do anything without me. I think he was manipulating me into feeling the same — that I shouldn't want to do anything without him, either. It worked. Eventually, my life was very limited. I had to sneak calls to my friends to discuss new recipes or regular homework. If Marco called and my line was busy, he'd ask me about it the next day. I'd tell him my mother was on the phone. I had to memorize recipes after he left the house — he didn't like me doing that when he was around. He'd never help me prepare for my tests. He never wanted to taste anything I'd made at school. My world was smaller than an ant's.

What Do You Think?

1. Why is it easier to control a person by keeping her from seeing her friends?

2. Why didn't Marco ever consider what Juanita wanted? Why do you think Juanita let her goals be pushed aside and ignored?

3. Why did Juanita think that Marco's jealousy was cool?

4. Have you ever had a boyfriend who followed you around or showed up unexpectedly? If so, how did that feel? Was it cool or creepy? Why?

Things to Do

1. Ask a friend if she's ever had a boyfriend who behaved like Marco.

2. If your friend doesn't know the signs of emotional abuse, explain them to her.
3. Find out if your state has antistalking laws. If it does, try to get a copy of the laws (some states have Web sites where you can look up laws). Reading these laws will help you understand exactly what behaviors are illegal.

Keeping a Journal

Write down how you would react if you had a boyfriend who was emotionally abusive.

4 Verbal Abuse

> I come from a pretty soft-spoken family, so when Jed began yelling at me and criticizing me, it was hard to take. I made excuses for his abuse and even rationalized it. I told myself that he was being honest by saying what he really felt. It took almost six months before I realized that I was being verbally abused. By the time I ended it, I was feeling pretty low about myself.
>
> —Brittany, 14

Verbal abuse includes frequent criticism, put-downs, ridicule, threats, and yelling. Almost anybody can get verbally abusive sometimes. But if, like Jed, your dating partner criticizes or puts you down often or whenever he seems upset, he is verbally abusive. (Some people consider all kinds of verbal abuse another form of emotional abuse.)

Some parents are verbally abusive, too. Just because Mom or Dad are really critical or verbally abusive in other ways doesn't mean that it's okay or that you have to accept this treatment from a boyfriend as well.

Criticism

Brittany wanted to be a cheerleader. She liked clothes and she liked to shop. She had lots of friends and would spend the weekends hanging out at the mall with them. She thought that maybe she'd like to be a fashion designer and spent a lot of her time looking through fashion magazines, and designing and making her own clothes.

Brittany's boyfriend Jed said the sweetest things to her at first.

He was the nicest boyfriend I'd ever had. He was so polite. He complimented me on my clothes. He loved my fashion designs. I just melted when he looked at me. That didn't last for long.

I know that there is good criticism and bad criticism. Good criticism is really helpful, and the person giving it is trying to be positive. Telling you doesn't necessarily give the person pleasure or personal benefit. Bad criticism doesn't build you up. It tears you down.

Does your dating partner criticize you a lot? Does he find fault with what you do or say, especially things you used to think you did pretty well?

Jed began making negative comments about practically everything — my makeup, my clothes, the colors I chose. If I was even one minute late, he'd criticize me. He even criticized how I said hi to him on the phone. It got so that even things I was proud of, Jed would criticize those, too. I felt that nothing I did or said would pass Jed's inspection.

Name-calling

Name-calling is when a person uses a one-word or two-word name that is negative and intended to be hurtful.

At times, when Jed didn't want me to do my homework, he'd call me a "stuck-up suck-up" or "Miss Superior." When he really wanted to get to me, he'd call me a "retard" or a "spaz," especially when I had to go to cheerleading practice.

Put-downs

Put-downs are a kind of criticism that attacks the whole person. Criticisms are more specific.

Jed would say things like "You can't draw," "You're dumb," "You're fat." It seemed like he didn't like anything about me, even though he kept going out with me.

Ridicule

Ridicule is when a person tries to get other people to laugh at someone and makes himself feel bigger, better, or more popular at the other person's expense.

One time Jed and I were sitting at a table with a bunch of friends. In front of everyone, he told me I had so much makeup on I looked like a hooker. Most of the guys laughed. When I didn't laugh, Jed told me that not only did I look like a hooker, but also I didn't have a sense of humor.

Ridicule mocks and taunts you. It makes you feel humiliated and embarrassed. It turns you into a joke.

Discounting

If your date "disses" something you say or your feelings or something you do, that's discounting and disrespect. You feel like nothing you say, feel, or do is of any importance.

After a while, Jed told me I didn't feel sad when I had just told him I did feel sad. If I told him I was angry with him, he would tell me that I really wasn't angry with him. I helped him with his homework once and felt pretty good about it. Later he said he really didn't need my help.

Verbal Threats

Any verbal threat of harm by a date is abusive. A common one is to threaten to leave the relationship or to hurt you or himself.

Whenever he didn't get his way, Jed threatened to break up with me. If I didn't do certain things he wanted or if I ever showed that I wasn't happy with him, he told me that if I did or said that again, he would hurt me. If I suggested that maybe we weren't right for each other, he'd threaten to kill himself. It got so I was just tense and afraid around him.

The intent of a verbal threat is to control your behavior in some way.

Yelling and Screaming

When a dating partner yells or screams at you (unless it is to get you out of immediate physical danger), this is the most obvious kind of verbal abuse. Nobody enjoys being yelled at.

When he yelled and screamed at me, his face got red, his eyes bulged, and his veins stuck out. And it was over the smallest things! At times I thought he was a second away from hitting me. I realized that Jed was scary like that.

It's hard to feel good about yourself when somebody yells and screams at you. Yelling and screaming are not kind or loving, nor are they helpful ways of communicating when you are trying to solve problems. A healthy dating relationship is kind, loving, safe, and fun. There may be disagreements in a healthy relationship, even passionate ones, but they are not screaming matches, and even when a partner questions your beliefs or reasons, he doesn't verbally attack you as a person.

What Do You Think?

1. What's different (if anything) when your boyfriend ridicules you and when a male classmate you hardly know ridicules you?

2. Why do you think Jed's negative comments bothered Brittany so much, even though she knew that most of them weren't true?

3. Is there anything about Brittany's comments that remind you of a relationship you've been in? What were the criticisms? Did you believe them? Why?

Things to Do

1. Keep track of any examples of verbal abuse you overhear at school or when you're out with your friends.

2. When you're watching movies or TV, watch for dialogue that includes verbal abuse. Keep track of how many times you hear it for a week.

3. Underneath most verbal abuse is anger. When you go to the movies, watch for scenes of verbal abuse. Be alert for the anger behind most displays of verbal abuse.

Keeping a Journal

Has anyone ever been verbally abusive to you? Write down what's been said to you, when it happened, how you felt, and what you did about it.

5 Physical Abuse

Terrell is a jock. I'm pretty tough myself. I've played soccer since third grade. My team won State last year. I've already been scouted by some colleges. I knew my friend Cathy had been hit pretty bad by her boyfriend. That would never happen to me. No one could push me around. I wouldn't take crap from anyone. Until Terrell, that is.

—LaShawnda, 18

LaShawnda was a star on the soccer team and was used to physical contact. Over the years, she had had some serious athletic injuries, including two knee surgeries. She always came back and played harder. She wasn't afraid of getting hurt. Her teammates knew that she'd give everything to win. She was a leader.

LaShawnda began dating Terrell the summer before her senior year. Before long, he became physically abusive.

Physical abuse is the kind of abuse that makes the newspapers. Physical abuse causes clear harm or injury to the victim. Most physical abuse consists of illegal acts and can result in criminal charges against the abuser.

Physical abuse is intentional aggressive physical contact with another person, and it hurts. It's done on purpose, because somebody is angry or wants to control another person. Accidentally bumping into other kids in the hall is not physical abuse. Physical abuse hurts and often leaves marks. The behavior is usually deliberate, though the person being physically abusive may not always intend to hurt you. Pushing, shoving, grabbing, and pinning down are forms of physical abuse. Slapping, punching, choking, hitting, and threatening to use or using a lethal weapon are more serious. Physically abusive people can cause bruises, broken bones, head injuries, and death. Sometimes they only bruise, but sometimes they can kill you.

Physical abuse, like other forms of abuse, controls another person. Victims understandably get scared and change their speech and behaviors to try calm down or satisfy the abuser's demands.

Pushing, Shoving, Grabbing, Pinning Down

Terrell began to control LaShawnda by grabbing and pushing her.

It started when we argued. It didn't take much to set him off. Sometimes I did something he didn't like. Sometimes he didn't like it if I didn't give him my complete attention. The first time, he grabbed me real hard and pushed me towards the wall. The next day I noticed welts on my arm. If I had lighter skin it would have looked more discolored. As it was, I wore a sweater to cover up the welts. I didn't want anyone to think I let Terrell push me around.

I know what it's like to get angry. Sometimes you do things you wouldn't do ordinarily. Maybe I got too loud myself during the argument, so I blew it off.

The physical stuff continued. It happened mainly during an argument. I tried not to say things or do things that got him angry. After a while, there was no rhyme or reason. No matter what I did or said, he'd get angry and grab me.

I started to get scared. I'm all muscle and pretty big for a girl. But Terrell's six inches taller and outweighs me by almost 80 pounds. If he really wanted to hurt me bad, he could.

Often the abuser apologizes after he hurts you. Sometimes he tells you that if you would just not make him angry, everything would be okay. And sometimes he blames his anger on drinking or drugs or having a bad day. But often abusers consciously or unconsciously choose to drink or take drugs so they'll have an excuse to be out of control.

At first Terrell would apologize the next day. He told me he'd been drinking but loved me and would never hurt me. (*As if he hadn't just hurt me!*) Then he'd be real nice for a while.

The sweet times in between the blowups are what keep dating partners coming back to the relationship. The abuser apologizes and treats you very well for a while. Your dating partner may bring you a present or take you out for dinner or buy flowers, hoping you'll forgive and forget. Sometimes it works. This is called the "honeymoon phase."

> Later it got to where he never even apologized. He'd just say that I needed to try harder to be nice, not make him angry. He told me he had lots of pressures and I shouldn't add to his pressures.

Sometimes grabbing, pushing, and shoving can lead to more serious, if unintended, kinds of physical abuse. These behaviors can hurt you and lead to serious injury, intended or not. You can lose your balance or fall and hit your head. Severe injury or death sometimes happens.

> One time Terrell pushed me during an argument and I fell down the stairs. My ankle was sprained so bad I couldn't play in the game against South. I could have broken my arm or leg and been out longer. My coach suspected what had happened and told me I'd better get help. As I stood on the sidelines, I realized falling down stairs is a good way to get myself killed.

> Terrell said that he was surprised I fell down the stairs. He claimed he hardly even pushed me. Who's he kidding? He said he never meant to hurt me, he just wanted to get my attention. I felt humiliated. I didn't want to face anyone.

Regardless of his intentions (and we know that his intention is to control you), pushing and shoving put you in danger. What matters is that you have been seriously injured as a result of something your dating partner has done.

> I should have broken up with Terrell then, but I convinced myself that he didn't mean to hurt me. I didn't want to think I couldn't handle this. I still wouldn't admit to myself that he was abusive.

Slapping, Hitting, Punching, Choking, and Threatening to Use or Using a Lethal Weapon

Even when the abuser claims he didn't intend to hurt you, the fact is that injury is the logical result of these behaviors. Injuries can range from faint bruises to lost teeth to broken bones (often broken facial bones, sometimes requiring painful reconstructive surgery) to death. Abusers promise that they will never hurt you again. They almost never keep their promises without spending time in a treatment program for abusers or a treatment program for people with anger problems.

> I was able to tell Terrell that I wasn't going to be pushed around anymore. He agreed. I really loved him, but I didn't like how he treated me. Things went pretty well for two weeks. Then one night he blew up at me and punched me in the face and head. I heard the bones crack before I passed out.

> When I came to at the hospital I had tubes going in and out of me and was hooked up to all sorts of monitors. They told me that he had broken my jaw. I had had surgery and my jaw was wired shut. The punch to my head caused a contusion and a concussion. I had been unconscious for two days.

I spent six nights in the hospital — two days in intensive care and four days in neuro-rehab. The docs were concerned about permanent brain damage.

Terrell called me at the hospital. Since I couldn't talk, my mother spoke with him. He apologized and cried. He begged me not to do anything — like press charges — and he promised it would never happen again.

Being laid up in the hospital helped in a weird way. It gave me time to think. I realized that Terrell was abusive and that, as bad as my injuries were, I was alive. If I wanted to stay alive, I'd have to leave Terrell. He couldn't keep his promises because he was completely out of control.

I had my mother call the police from my hospital bed and I filed charges against Terrell. They arrested him for assault. I felt bad about sending him to jail because I still loved him, and Terrell always said that the way he acted was _my_ fault. Can you _believe_ it? I had to work to convince myself that I didn't deserve to be crapped on like this. I matter. If I don't matter enough to me to save my own life, then who am I going to matter to?

It was hard to leave him because I really loved him. I thought he loved me, too. But he never took any responsibility for his anger or how he hurt me, the damage he caused. Even when he apologized, he suggested that it was still somehow my fault. My self-esteem was shot. My friends couldn't believe I'd let him hurt me. It took months to get over Terrell. There were times when I thought I'd call him in jail. I was very close to going back to him. I had to keep reminding myself how much pain I was in after my jaw surgery and from my head injuries. And how I might have died. I had to keep remembering how humiliated and scared I was around him.

If anything like this ever happens to you, like my coach said, you better get some help.

What Do You Think?

1. Terrell would sometimes be nice after he'd been physically abusive to LaShawnda. Then he'd abuse her again. Why do you think this cycle or pattern happens?

2. Do you think LaShawnda would still be seeing Terrell if he hadn't broken her jaw? Why? Why not?

3. Why do you think pushing and shoving should be considered signs of physical abuse?

Things to Do

1. Look up in a library or search the Internet to find information on the different types or degrees (first degree, second degree, and so on) of assault in your state's laws. If a person is convicted, how long are the jail or prison sentences for each type of assault? If you get a chance during school vacation, visit your city or county courthouse. Unless children are involved, domestic abuse cases are usually heard in open court and are open to the public. Or look in the newspaper for the court report and count how many cases of assault or endangerment are listed. Keep track for a month.

2. Ask a counselor at school how many incidents of physical abuse or assault between a girlfriend and boyfriend took place at school last year. Whatever figures you get, remember that they cover only reported incidents.

3. Call a shelter for women. See if you can find out what percentage of women there were physically abused by their boyfriends or husbands. Also ask whether the shelter has dealt with any cases of men being abused by their wives or girlfriends, or abusive partners in same-sex relationships.

Keeping a Journal

Write down what you think your reaction would be if your boyfriend hit you and broke your nose.

6 Sexual Abuse

I was only sixteen. I didn't think I was ready to have sex until I was a little older. Tyler was seventeen. He was my first serious boyfriend. It was all very romantic. He sent me flowers, left me love notes in my locker at school, and wrote me poems. My girlfriends were real impressed. I felt pretty grown up. Other boys would come on to me, but I let them know that Tyler was the only one I wanted to be with.

—Karina, 16

Karina had been dating Tyler for almost a year. It was all very romantic, sort of like the romance novels she read. He spent a lot of time with her. She had a part-time job after school working for a dog groomer. She really liked animals. So did Tyler. They seemed to have many things in common.

They did a lot of sexual touching and deep kissing but never had intercourse. She liked the closeness. Karina felt most loved by Tyler when they were physically close. He seemed more vulnerable and more real then.

Sexual abuse is when a boyfriend verbally pressures you or physically forces you to have sex, even though you have shown little interest in having sex or have said no.

Verbal Pressure

There are various ways to apply verbal pressure to have sex. A boyfriend may threaten to leave you or imply there's something wrong with you if you won't have sex.

We'd been dating for almost a year. I thought that he was happy with the way things were. I know I was happy. I felt like I could talk to him about anything. He really listened to me and understood me. We talked for hours about how much we loved animals. We'd fantasize about how we might work together as animal trainers after we graduated. I felt that he knew me very well. I loved him and he loved me. We even talked about how we might get married one day. I would daydream a lot about being married after high school.

Then Tyler began to pressure me to have sex. I told him I didn't feel ready for it yet. I was too young and I was afraid of getting pregnant or maybe some sexually transmitted disease I had studied in health class. He said that age has nothing to do with it and we would be safe as long as he used a condom. I tried to point out that accidents happen, but he just laughed. He said he wasn't a klutz and he knew how to use a condom. I said I didn't feel emotionally ready.

Several weeks later, he brought up sex again when we were making out. He told me that other girls my age were doing it, so what's my problem? He was right about that. I knew several girls who were having sex with their boyfriends. No matter how much I tried to tell him I wasn't ready, he wouldn't listen. He wouldn't take no for an answer. My feelings didn't count anymore.

Then, he switched his tactics. He said that if I really loved him as much as he loved me, I would have sex with him. He made it sound very noble, like if two people love each other, sex is the way to prove it. I told him that there were other ways to show my love besides having sex with him. I wish I'd thought of saying that the way for him to prove he loved me was to respect my feelings.

Every time we got together he pressured me. He didn't seem to care anymore about what I wanted. He only cared about what he wanted. Then he told me that I must be frigid and that he didn't want a girlfriend who didn't like sex. I heard this as a threat. I believed that if I didn't have sex with him, he would leave me. To tell the truth, I had begun to wonder if my reasons were good reasons or whether maybe I <u>was</u> frigid! I was tired of fighting. Finally, I gave in.

Your boyfriend may also pressure you to go beyond your comfort zone and have types of sex you're uncomfortable with or to drink or do drugs.

Once I gave in, all Tyler wanted to do was have sex. We didn't just talk or go to a movie or study or take the dogs for a walk anymore. Often sex with him hurt. My resentment never really went away. I still felt angry about all the pressure he put on me and how it changed our relationship. Maybe he sensed it, since he started suggesting we smoke pot beforehand. He said it would relax me. From then on, we'd do pot before sex. I think he was using other stuff, too.

Physical Force

Sex done against your will is rape, a serious form of sexual assault. You don't have to fight off your dating partner or show bruises for sex to be rape. If you say no or clearly indicate that you don't want to have sex and he forces you, that's rape. Sex with just the threat of force is also considered rape.

One night Tyler wanted to have sex. I had come home from school early because I didn't feel good. I told him I wasn't in the mood. Before I knew it, Tyler had my clothes off and had pinned me down. It really hurt, but he wouldn't stop. It was a long time before I realized he had raped me.

Date Rape

A unique and all too common kind of rape is called date rape. Date rape occurs when you and the attacker know each other and are on a date by choice. It could be your first date or your twentieth date, though it usually happens during one of the early dates, when the relationship is fairly casual. You say no. You don't want sex, and your date makes you have sex. It often happens so fast that you are caught off guard. Some date rapists have been known to get their dates drunk or to put drugs (such as "roofies" or "K" or "GHB") in their dates' drinks while they're in the bathroom or over talking to other friends for a few minutes. The girl gets drowsy or paralyzed or passes out. Amnesia is a common effect of these drugs, so victims may not even realize they were raped. There's more information on date rape drugs in Appendix D.

Date rape is always wrong. There are no good reasons for it. Some date rapists feel that they are entitled to sex, especially if they've put out some money for the date. In their minds, sex is the payoff for dinner and a concert.

Girls who are raped on a date often don't report it. They often blame themselves and think that other people won't believe them. Usually there are no bruises and no witnesses — it's just their word against the rapists' that they didn't want sex. The guys involved may threaten to harm them if they report the rape. Despite these factors, victims of date rape should always report it to the police, because it's the only way a rapist can be caught and stopped.

Remember, a good relationship is one in which each partner respects the feelings of the other. This kind of respect is especially important when it comes to something as intimate as sex. Verbal pressure or physical force to have sex is never a part of a healthy relationship.

What Do You Think?

1. At first, Tyler used verbal pressure to convince Karina to have sex with him. What kinds of verbal pressure would work with you? Why? Why not?

2. How could someone "prove" that he or she loves another person? What would be "enough" proof? Why do you think someone would ask for "proof"?

3. Can you think of other ways to show your love besides having sex? List five ways.

Things to Do

1. What were the various reasons Karina gave for not wanting to have sex with Tyler? What would be your reasons? Make a list. How could you counter the arguments of someone pressuring you to have sex? Make a list.

2. Sexual assault and date rape are fairly common. Read the newspaper, check the library's guide to periodicals, or take some library books out on sexual abuse and date rape. See if you can find out how many cases of sexual assault and date rape are reported in your state. However many are reported, remember that many, many more incidents of sexual assault and date rape are not reported.

Keeping a Journal

Write down why you think sex would be more enjoyable when both partners agree to have sex.

7 Why Abusers Abuse

I felt like a man when I controlled girls.

—Marco

Jerry, Marco, Jed, Terrell, and Tyler attend weekly group sessions, Terrell by speaker phone from jail. Each boy still finds it difficult to admit his abusive behavior and take responsibility for it. They still make excuses for their behavior. Occasionally, a couple of the boys seem able to admit that some of their behavior was abusive.

Marco: *Juanita kept telling me I was controlling her. I was afraid she'd leave me if I didn't have the upper hand.*

Jed: *I don't know what was happening to me. I found myself criticizing and yelling at Brittany all the time. I thought she was better than me, so I put her down a lot.*

Terrell: My father smacked my mother around quite a bit. She never complained. He had her under his thumb. Whenever I got angry with LaShawnda, it felt natural to smack her. I thought women like it when the man's the boss.

Jerry: I don't know why I'm here. I was never abusive. Ever.

Tyler: I was frustrated. I loved Karina. When people love each other, they have sex. She was just afraid of it. I knew once she did it, she'd love it. I bet she was glad I made her do it.

There are many reasons why abusers abuse.

Abusers like to have control over others. It makes them feel good, more secure, calmer. Some abusers need to have control only over their partners. Other abusers need to have control over all the people close to them.

Whenever abusers feel other people challenging their control or authority in some way, they become abusive. Their abuse can be emotional, verbal, physical, sexual, or a combination.

Marco: I felt strong when I controlled Juanita.

Jed: For a while, Brittany did whatever I wanted when I criticized her.

Many abusers have hot tempers. Their anger levels shoot up quickly. Until they learn ways to control their anger, they lash out verbally or physically. Sometimes they are completely out of control with rage, and they hurt the people they love. Sometimes they beat them up so badly they cause serious or fatal injuries. When they are not angry or frightened to the point of anger, some of these abusers can be sweet and gentle. After a display of anger, abusers often say, "I didn't mean to hurt you." A period of peace, calm, and sweetness often follows.

> Terrell: *I've always had a temper. When I pushed LaShawnda, I didn't mean for her to fall down the stairs. I felt bad she hurt herself. When I punched her, I was completely out of control. I can't stop myself when I get that angry. But she <u>made</u> me angry.*

Many abusers abuse alcohol and/or drugs. Alcohol and drugs can have different effects on people. For some people, they can heighten belligerence and aggression.

> Terrell: *I drank a lot. LaShawnda didn't always know. I was more likely to blow my top if I'd been drinking.*

For other abusers, alcohol and drugs may lower their inhibitions, causing them to act out certain behaviors they might not display if they weren't abusing alcohol or drugs.

> Tyler: *I told Karina she could relax more if she did pot. When I did pot and used some coke, I felt like I could take on ten girls at the same time. There was nothing I couldn't do!*

Abusers often blame drugs or alcohol for their behavior but make no effort to stop using them. Some abusers, in fact, use their drug of choice — alcohol, marijuana (pot, grass, weed, dope), cocaine (coke, crack) — to make it easier for them to abuse their victims. The drug or drink erases any feeling of guilt or shame about what they're doing to hurt someone else.

Some abusers have low self-esteem. But more often, abusers have what is called "fragile high self-esteem." Their self-esteem — the way they feel about themselves — is linked to how other people in their lives regard them or how much approval they get from others. A person with fragile high self-esteem is sensitive to any sign that someone is criticizing or perhaps rejecting him or her. Feeling rejected is so threatening to the person that he or she lashes out to feel more in control, more secure.

> Terrell: *I've got lots of awards for football. People always admired me. I needed their admiration. Whenever I thought LaShawnda thought less of me, I could feel myself getting tense and angry.*

> Tyler: *All the girls before Karina thought I was a hunk. They fought over me. Karina didn't seem to appreciate me like the others. She even implied that I didn't know how to use a condom!*

Some abusers do have low self-esteem. They have to put down or dominate others in some way in order to feel better about themselves.

> Marco: *I don't know why, but by controlling Juanita, I felt better about myself.*

> Jed: *Brittany was successful in so many ways. She really knew clothes and fashion. I couldn't believe that she could see anything special about me. I needed to show her that she wasn't so perfect. Somehow I felt less stupid when I criticized her.*

For some abusers, abuse is a learned response. They may have seen men abuse their mothers. Maybe abuse is all they've ever seen. Some abusive boys have seen their fathers treat their mothers like property. They've learned to believe, "She's mine. I can do anything I want to her." They've learned to act in abusive ways when there is any kind of disagreement or conflict, when they become angry, or when they feel threatened or stressed.

When a boyfriend's male role models have been abusive, he may think that abuse is the right way — or the only way — to act toward a female.

> Terrell: *Most men are rough with their women. My father and his brothers all smacked their women around. That's how you control them. Put the fear of God in them.*

> Marco: *My father was always yelling and screaming at my mother. We were all afraid of him.*

Some abusers have been abused themselves. There is evidence that some abusers were physically, emotionally, or sexually abused as children. They reenact their own abuse, this time with themselves in the powerful role of abuser. This is partly a learned response. They have learned to treat others the same way they were treated.

> Marco: *My dad wanted to know where my sisters were every minute. He wouldn't let my sisters have boyfriends. He kept them on a tight leash. He didn't control me as much, but I don't think he trusted me.*

> Terrell: *My father hit me and my brothers. I've been angry ever since. I told myself that if anyone even so much as looked at me wrong, watch out. No one is going to hurt me, in any way, again.*

Some abusers are emotionally unbalanced. They act out their violent thoughts in violent ways. These abusers often have long histories of violence. Some become murderers. As children, they were cruel and violent toward animals and people and seemed to *enjoy* their cruel acts.

This type of abuser is very dangerous. Marco, Jed, Jerry, and Tyler do not fit this profile. We can't be sure about Terrell at this point.

What Do You Think?

1. All the girls at some point realized that their boyfriends were abusive. They also realized that their boyfriends felt a need to control them. Why do you think each boyfriend abused his girlfriend?

2. If a boy has a controlling father, how do you think he will try to control his girlfriend?

3. Do you think all boys who are abusive have self-esteem problems? Should it matter? What's the difference between having feelings and acting out those feelings?

4. Would you want a boyfriend who tried to control you? Why? Why not?

5. Did any of these boys take responsibility for their abuse? Review what they said and underline any statements in which they admit that the abuse was their fault. Circle any statements made by the boys that blame the girls they dated for their violence. How many responsible statements did you find? How many blaming statements?

Things to Do

Ask your girlfriends if they have ever had boyfriends who were bossy and controlling. Ask them what some of the controlling behaviors were.

Keeping a Journal

1. Have you ever been around a boy with a hot temper? Write down how it felt when he blew up.

2. How do you usually react when someone tries to control you? Write about it.

8

Effects of Abuse on Victims

I was a pretty spontaneous and chatty person. After being with Jed for a while, where nothing I said or did was right, I became quiet, like a mouse.

— Brittany

If you've been in an abusive relationship or have friends who have been in that situation, you may recognize some or all of the effects of abuse on the victim. Different people exposed to the same abuse pattern may react very differently.

Most victims either don't realize or deny that what they are experiencing is abuse; most deny that the abusive behavior is serious enough to seek help or get out of the relationship.

Juanita: *At first, I didn't realize Marco was so controlling. I thought it was his way of caring.*

LaShawnda: *When Terrell first pushed me, I didn't think much of it. Even when I fell down the stairs, a part of me didn't see how dangerous he was.*

A person who is "in denial" (pretends that something isn't happening) usually either *minimizes* or *excuses* the abuser's behavior. Minimizing is thinking that the behavior wasn't as bad as it really was or that, because the abuser says he didn't do it on purpose, it's not really so bad. Excusing and *rationalizing* are ways of thinking up reasons that the behavior is not the person's fault or is somehow okay because of circumstances. We all rationalize some things, such as how much we *need* new sneakers when we really just *want* them. But rationalizing dangerous behavior puts us in harm's way.

LaShawnda: *I didn't think Terrell meant to push me down the stairs. He told me afterwards that he didn't mean for me to fall down the stairs.*

Brittany: *Sometimes when Jed yelled at me, I just told myself that he'd had a bad day.*

People being victimized often blame themselves. They feel as if they're at fault, or they accept it when the abuser tells them it's their fault. They don't hold the abuser responsible for his behavior.

LaShawnda: *When Terrell got angry, I felt I was to blame. If I could just be sweeter to him, he wouldn't get angry. Even when I fell down the stairs, I believed it was my fault. I'm an athlete — I should have been able to break my fall.*

Brittany: Of course it was my fault. Jed told me so a hundred times.

Karina: I thought I was to blame. Tyler had a right to expect sex after we'd been going together all that time.

Some people being victimized feel that they provoked the abuser's behavior. Or they accept it when the abuser tells them that they provoked the abuse.

Brittany: I felt that I set Jed off. If only I could learn how to sweet-talk, he'd be nicer to me.

LaShawnda: When I tried to sort of talk to him about his anger, he'd fly off the handle. Trying to bring stuff up made it worse. I don't think Terrell would have become so angry if I had just shut my mouth.

In some cases, people being victimized do provoke their abusive partners. Sometimes they know the explosion is coming and just want to get it over with. Those partners must be responsible for their behavior as well. But no matter what any person in a relationship does that might be provoking, no one deserves to be abused. There are always other options. It's always a choice to walk away and do something to chill out without hurting anyone: shoot some hoops, run a mile, take the mountain bike up a steep trail, do some chores, throw rocks in the woods or at the lake or in the dump.

Many victims have low self-esteem and self-worth. When these people stay in abusive relationships, their low self-esteem is reinforced by their abusive partners.

Juanita: I never felt very good about myself. I thought Marco was the best thing that happened to me.

It's a cycle of feeling bad about yourself, then being hit or yelled at or sexually pressured or assaulted, then feeling worse. The abuser says it's your fault, and you feel like you're not worth anything and no one else will want you, so you stay with the partner who makes you feel bad.

> Juanita: *I'm not worth anything. Marco abuses me. So that proves I'm not worth anything.*

Victims with low self-esteem have convinced themselves that no decent boy will ever be interested in them, so they accept the boyfriends they do have, even if they are abusive.

> Juanita: *I thought a guy like Marco was the best I could get. Ay!*

When someone with low self-esteem stays in an abusive relationship, her self-esteem sinks even lower.

Some people who are abused get into a cycle of retaliation. Instead of getting out, they fight back indirectly with words or mind games. Because he yelled at her, she doesn't talk to him for two days, for example. They become passive-aggressive — they express their resentment and anger in indirect or passive ways, instead of confronting the abusive behavior directly: "Stop yelling at me. I didn't do anything wrong. Your bad mood is not my fault." When both dating partners behave abusively, watch out! The dating relationship becomes explosive.

Victims who fear their partners try to modify their own behaviors to calm the abusive partner. Eventually, the girl can no longer be herself in the relationship. She talks or behaves in ways that she thinks will help her avoid abuse.

Brittany: I found myself trying to calm Jed down all the time. I'd try to read his moods so I wouldn't say something upsetting at the wrong time. It was like dodging bullets.

LaShawnda: I'd try to think before I spoke. If only I could say the right thing, maybe Terrell wouldn't get angry. Early on, I thought I saw a pattern. I thought I was able to keep him calm. Later, there was no pattern. Just me breathing could set him off.

Karina: He had been so sensitive to what I had to say. Interested in my interests. I thought he'd understand and still love me even if I didn't want to have sex. Wrong! If it was in his plans for the evening, he'd make me have sex one way or another.

Victims often develop emotional problems. They may be tense, exhibit anxiety symptoms, or become depressed.

Brittany: I'd bitten my fingernails to the cuticles. I wasn't sleeping well anymore.

LaShawnda: It wasn't until I stopped seeing Terrell that I realized I'd been depressed for months.

Karina: I wasn't myself anymore. My grades slipped. I was tense all the time. I was afraid of Tyler. I wanted to throw up, and I didn't feel like eating.

People in abusive relationships try to justify staying. When asked why they didn't leave the relationship, girls in abusive dating relationships give various reasons.

Juanita: I loved him. I was afraid he'd hurt me if I left.

Brittany: When he wasn't yelling at me or criticizing, Jed was wonderful.

LaShawnda: I was afraid to leave him. He threatened to kill me if I left him.

Karina: When he wasn't pressuring me to have sex, he was kind and gentle. I was afraid that no one would want me after him — that he'd tell other guys that he'd had sex with me and that's all they'd want from me. I kept thinking about how he was in the beginning and hoping it would be that way again.

Cathy: I was too ashamed to leave. I didn't want anyone to know that Jerry abused me.

People who are being victimized often feel powerless to help themselves. They are in a cycle of negative thinking and behavior. They feel paralyzed and helpless to do anything to get out. They often become deeply depressed and don't see any way out. The abuser's control over their lives has created what feels like a prison with no windows and no door.

Brittany: For the longest time, I felt paralyzed. I couldn't think straight. Jed pulled me down so far that I believed what he said about me for the longest time. I was this worthless, fat, insensitive bitch. He told me that often enough.

Juanita: Marco had me so controlled, so under his thumb that I couldn't think for myself. I wasn't happy, but I was too depressed to do much about getting out.

Some victims are desperate to be loved. Even though they are being treated badly, they cling to the abuser because they think the abuser loves them. Girls fear that if they leave the relationship, they may never find another boy to love them.

> Cathy: That was me. I needed Jerry's love. Without it, I was nothing; I felt empty when he wasn't around. I guess I was willing to be abused in exchange for love. Besides, I had to have a boyfriend!

Some victims become dependent on the abuser. They can't imagine themselves living without the abuser. They stay with him no matter how abusively they are treated.

> Juanita: I was absolutely dependent on Marco. Part of that was me, my needs. Part of it was Marco. He'd convince me that I should be dependent on him, let him make all the decisions, tell me what to do. My excitement about being a chef was gone. I had no confidence that I could do anything myself.

> Cathy: For a while I never did much without consulting Jerry — even things I'd done perfectly well before he came into the picture. I lost all my independence.

Victims feel trapped and alone. Abusers have victims so controlled and isolated from friends and family that they feel there is no one to turn to.

> Juanita: There was no one to help me get out — at least that's how I felt.

What Do You Think?

1. Why do you think abuse victims deny or try to minimize the seriousness of the abuser's behavior?

2. Of the five girls you read about here, which girl do you feel was in the most denial? Why did you choose her?

3. Were you surprised to see LaShawnda putting up with Terrell's behavior?

4. Which of the effects of abuse mentioned in this chapter seem the most damaging? Why?

Things to Do

If you have a friend who was in an abusive dating relationship, ask her what some of the effects of the abuse were.

Keeping a Journal

1. If you were ever in an abusive dating relationship, write down how that relationship affected you.

2. If you haven't been in an abusive dating relationship, see if you can imagine how dating someone like Jerry (Cathy's boyfriend) would affect you. Write down your thoughts.

9
Eleven Manipulations Abusers Use

Even though she gave me a million chances, I always thought I deserved more because I loved her.

—Marco

Abusers always justify and make excuses for their behavior. Abusive behavior cannot be justified. When abusers defend their abuse, it is clear that they're not taking responsibility for what they've done.

When victims try to talk with abusers about their behavior, abusers often respond with these predictable lines. As you read them, think about how many times you've heard them from someone you know.

1. "I didn't mean to hurt you."

Some abusers' behavior is so out of control that it may be true that they didn't mean to hurt you, but they do mean to control you. Focus on the results of the behavior, not just on the intent. If the result is that you have been hurt, recognize the danger of future abuse. Your partner may hurt you again, whether he means to or not.

> Terrell: I told LaShawnda a zillion times that I didn't mean to hurt her. I thought I really meant it. She believed me at first.

> Jerry: Cathy told me that sex hurt her. I didn't mean to hurt her. I thought once she saw how great sex was, she'd love it.

2. "I won't do it again."

Some abusers apologize, especially after they have hurt you physically or forced you sexually, and they promise not to do it again. But abusers feel such a need to control others that their abusive behavior has become a habit. Their abuse of you is probably not a one-time thing, and it's probably not the first time they've abused a girlfriend. Despite their promises not to do it again, the chances are nearly 100 percent that they will. Girls in abusive relationships learn that words are cheap. Their boyfriends make and break the same promises over and over.

> Terrell: After LaShawnda fell down the stairs, I felt really bad. I promised her it would never happen again. Even after I broke her jaw and punched her in the head, I tried to tell her it would never happen again.

> Jerry: I made tons of promises to Cathy that I would treat her differently after I began hitting her.

> Marco: At first, when Juanita tried to talk to me about how I criticized her, I promised I wouldn't do it again. No matter what I promised, the words would just come out. I must have broken my promise 50 million times. And she put up with it.

3. "If you leave me, I'll kill myself."

Because abuse is about control, abusers tend to be manipulative and will use any means to bend their dating partners to do what they want. Threatening to kill themselves if you leave them is a common threat. It is a form of verbal abuse designed to control your behavior. Your dating partner assumes that you won't leave because you're afraid that he may commit suicide if you do. No one would want that kind of guilt and responsibility — and no one who is truly loving would put that kind of responsibility on the person he loves.

> Jed: Yeah, I really had Brittany frightened with that one. I'm sure there were times I was so out of it that she thought I'd kill myself right in front of her.

> Marco: I was so dependent on Juanita that I said that to her many times. No matter what I did, she really thought she was responsible for it. No way she was going to leave me! Actually, there were times I even thought to myself, if she left me, I'd kill her first, then kill myself.

4. "You made me do it."

Abusers rarely, if ever, take responsibility for their behavior or admit that anything is their own fault. When they are abusive, they excuse their behavior by saying that something you did or said "made" them yell at you or put you down or hit you or sexually assault you. They try to make you believe that their abusive behavior is your fault!

Terrell: *I said it before, LaShawnda said things that set me off.*

Jerry: *Cathy said her homework was important. She could get Cs without doing her homework. She needed to learn that I was more important than her damn homework. She made me angry at her. That's why I hit her.*

Marco: *Juanita didn't want me to be in charge. She'd question my decisions. That made me want to control her even more. If only she'd leave things alone. I'd be fine then.*

Tyler: *Karina was such a tease. We'd kiss and touch and then she wouldn't go ahead and do it. If she hadn't led me on, I wouldn't have made her have sex with me.*

5. "You always dwell on the negative."

The abuser accuses you of focusing only on the problems of your relationship, not on the good stuff. He turns the situation around so that the problem isn't his abusive behavior — according to him, the problem is that you are "so negative," because you bring up his abusive behavior.

Jed: Brittany would nag me all the time about what I said to her. She could really ruin the mood. If she would just forget the bad stuff, it would've been okay. I was nice to her a lot. We had lots of good times.

Tyler: Karina never appreciated my good qualities. She never said anything nice about sex with me.

6. "If you just do what I say, things will be okay."

With this statement, the abuser again turns the problem around. Instead of taking responsibility for his behavior, he suggests that if you behave differently, he won't behave badly, and everything will be fine.

Jerry: I just wanted things my way. Whenever Cathy didn't obey me, I'd get angry. Just because I wanted to be in charge doesn't mean I was abusive.

Jed: I believed that what I did was right. Brittany had to learn not to question me.

7. "You always exaggerate."

Abusers deny that there could be anything wrong with them or their behavior. They minimize what they have done. It's easier for them to get away with it when their abuse does not involve physical endangerment. It is more difficult for them to claim that you exaggerate when the physical and sexual abuse is more serious. Abusers don't take responsibility for their behavior. They make you think it's your problem because you "exaggerate."

Jerry: *I felt Cathy thought I was the worst thing in her life. Whatever I did, she made it seem like I was trying to hurt her. How could I hurt her if I loved her? I don't understand.*

Terrell: *LaShawnda always made things bigger than they were. When she fell down the stairs, you'd think that I'd plotted to do that for weeks. She tried to make me feel guilty for pushing her!*

Tyler: *Karina said that sex would be better if I didn't pressure her. I just sweet-talked her. That's what guys have to do when girls aren't interested. She always exaggerated.*

8. "I don't yell at (or hit or push or sexually pressure) anyone else."

Abusers are always looking for someone else to blame for their behavior. With this statement, they imply that it must be your fault. For some abusers, the abuse is "person specific," that is, it only has to do with you, since they claim that there is no one else toward whom they behave abusively. Therefore, it must be something about you that "drives" them to behave so badly. They limit their abusive behavior to their dating partners or someone they are very close to.

The abuser suggests that there must be something about you or something you are doing or not doing that "causes" him to abuse you. Don't buy this line. It's just an excuse, a sign that he is not ready to look at his behavior and take responsibility for it. Some abusers actually lie when they say this. They have also been abusive with other girlfriends, but since you don't know about it, they can lie and get away with it.

Terrell: *A lot of times, I'd say anything that popped into my head to make LaShawnda think it was her fault. I'd hit other girls before, but I didn't love them the way I loved LaShawnda.*

Jed: *I'd never yelled at any other girl I was dating. I thought there was something about Brittany that made me yell at her. It was just another of my many excuses. I got very good at this. I was a pro.*

9. "You're crazy."

This manipulation makes you the problem, rather than the abusive behavior. It's another way for abusers to deny that they're doing anything wrong.

Marco: *I'd never had a girl question my behavior. Juanita would be so nice one minute but act very upset the next. I thought she was crazy. I learned later she was afraid of me.*

10. "You deserve it."

Abusers want you to think that their behavior is in some way okay. With this manipulation, they shift responsibility for their behavior to you. They justify their abusive behavior by saying that you deserve it.

No one deserves to be abused. Even if your behavior is inappropriate or you do something your partner doesn't like, he shouldn't abuse you. A loving dating partner should talk with you about it or take a time-out to cool off. If the situation can't be resolved, the two of you should decide to end the relationship.

Tyler: I said this a lot to Karina. I really thought she deserved it. I thought when she said no she meant yes. After all, she would make herself look sexy, so why shouldn't I respond?

11. "Do you think you can find anyone better?"

The abuser takes advantage of any doubts you may have about yourself. Often girls are so deep in an abusive relationship that it is difficult to think that anyone else would ever want them.

Terrell: Everyone thought I walked on water, including LaShawnda. She knew it would be a step down after me.

What Do You Think?

1. How easily can you be manipulated?

2. Which of the 11 manipulations mentioned in this chapter do you think you are most vulnerable to? Why? How can you "vaccinate" yourself against these manipulations?

3. Abusers say that if you just do what they want, everything will be okay. Why is this a manipulation? Is it successful?

4. Abusers resist taking responsibility for their behavior. They prefer to say that their behavior is their girlfriends' fault. Why is this a manipulation? Why does it work sometimes?

5. What's the worst thing that can happen if you end a relationship when your dating partner is being abusive?

Things to Do

1. List the ways you feel you've been manipulated in the past.

2. If you have girlfriends who have been in abusive relationships, ask them about the ways their boyfriends manipulated them. What behaviors did they use? Which ones were more successful? Are there other manipulations not mentioned here?

3. Read a book about "con games" and how they are played.

Keeping a Journal

Write down how it felt when someone tried to manipulate you.

Eleven Reasons Why Girls Stay

People looked at me differently when I started dating him. All the girls were jealous of me. Boys who never even knew I existed said hi in the halls. I couldn't let anyone know he was abusive. I don't think anyone would have believed me.

—Cathy

People in abusive dating relationships make mistakes in their thinking that allow them to stay in the relationship way too long. These ways of thinking about what's going on are called "thinking errors." Thinking errors are the things you say to yourself that somehow make the abuse you experience seem less important, less harmful, or less serious than it really is. When you catch yourself thinking these things and correct them, it is easier to see what's really going on and to get out of a bad situation.

1. "I finally was popular. I was afraid I'd be a nobody if I left him."

The rewards of being popular because of the person they're dating prompts many girls to remain with their abusers. They worry that their own reputations will suffer after a breakup.

> LaShawnda: *Terrell was the most popular guy in the school. I was a jock. People thought I could handle anything, that I didn't take crap from anyone. How could I tell them Terrell hurt me?*

> Brittany: *All my friends thought Jed was Romeo. They told me how lucky I was. Little did they know that Romeo was all an act and that the rest of the time he was yelling and screaming at me and putting me down.*

2. "I can handle this. He won't hurt me."

Girls often start out confident and independent. They tell themselves that they can handle any situation.

> Cathy: *Until Jerry hit me, I thought I was able to deal with him. I was able to avoid an argument or get him to relax. I thought in time I'd get better at it. I never thought he'd hit me.*

> LaShawnda: *I thought I was pretty tough, used to dissing guys who thought they were hot stuff. A guy once grabbed me in the hall and I got him good in his privates. He never tried that*

again. That all changed with Terrell. I still don't understand how I let him control me like he did.

Karina: Even when Tyler forced me to have sex, I still thought that I could handle it. I thought it was a one-time thing. He never really understood that sex was different for me.

Some girls tell themselves that as long as their boyfriends haven't hit them yet, it'll never happen. Studies show that an abuser's behavior often begins with emotional abuse and escalates from there.

3. "I understand him. I can help him change."

Partners in abusive relationships think that they can change the abuser. They try to analyze and treat the abuser so that he'll change. The answer to that thinking error is that the only person you can change is yourself. The other person has to want to change and has to take responsibility for his behavior. It takes time and effort — and often help from a trained counselor or therapist. As long as an abuser is getting what he wants from the abusive behavior, he doesn't have much of a reason to change.

Karina: I understood Tyler. I thought that since I knew all about him, what made him tick, that I could change him. I was so involved trying to understand him that I lost sight of my feelings. I would minimize the fact that he was forcing me to have sex. He showed no respect for my feelings!

Brittany: I had a class in human relations the year before. I kept trying to explain to Jed why he was being so nasty to me. I wanted to help him change.

4. "If he begins to lose control, I can calm him down."

Partners who are being abused often think that they can stop the abuser from getting out of control. Unfortunately, abusers can go from mild irritation to throwing punches or forcing you sexually in a matter of seconds. Few victims can calm an abuser down that quickly — or at all — when the abuser has decided that yelling, hitting, or sex is what's going to happen that day.

> LaShawnda: *When Terrell hit me, it came out of nowhere. It must have happened when I blinked my eyes. Really. If I'd seen it coming I would have done something to protect myself.*

> Karina: *It happened so fast. One minute I thought I was having a fairly calm discussion with Tyler, and the next minute my clothes were off and Tyler was in me. There was no stopping him.*

5. "I have to learn not to do or say anything to make him angry."

The person who is being abused in a relationship usually thinks that it's up to her to figure out how not to "set off" the abuser. But in fact, the abuser has already decided what will happen and is just looking for any excuse to explode.

> Brittany: *I thought I was the problem. I just wasn't reading him right. I thought if I learned to start our conversations differently, he wouldn't criticize me.*

> Cathy: *I was convinced I could control Jerry's temper. I was sure it had something to do with me. I even tried that "I-message"*

stuff we learned in school. Eventually I realized that controlling Jerry's temper wasn't my responsibility. Jerry was responsible for his behavior.

6. "All I need to do is make myself match his expectations of the ideal girl."

Girls can twist themselves like pretzels trying to meet abusers' expectations, which are usually not realistic. Some abusers change their expectations abruptly in order to maintain their control by keeping their victims off-balance.

> Juanita: I thought I knew what he wanted in a woman. Then I would behave or dress that way. Then he'd change his mind. A color he'd previously hated on me, now he wanted me to wear. A dish I had made a month before that he loved, he now said was terrible. It was like trying to hit a moving target. I could never please him, no matter how hard I tried.

7. "He doesn't mean it."

Abused partners use this thinking error because they can't believe they deserve such awful treatment. If they don't deserve it, the only other explanation is that it wasn't intentional or that the abuser didn't mean it or was just having a bad day. Also, some abusers say, "I didn't mean it. I just had a bad day at school" after they've been abusive, and their victims want to believe them. When you love a person, it's easy to make excuses for his behavior. In some instances, the abuser may not have meant to hurt you. However, most abusers do mean to control you, whether or not they are aware of it or admit it, and if it takes pain or forced sex to do it, then that's the method they'll use.

Girls and women in abusive relationships must really think about how the abuser treats them. An abuser might fatally injure his girlfriend and honestly say that he never meant to kill her. But she's just as dead, whether he meant to kill her or not.

> LaShawnda: *Whether or not Terrell meant to hurt me doesn't matter. When someone his size throws a punch, it's going to hurt, believe me.*

> Cathy: *Every time he'd hurt me, Jerry would always tell me he didn't mean it. But I think he hit me to keep me in line.*

8. "He's just having a bad day. I need to figure out when he's in a bad mood and not provoke him."

This is another thinking error that makes the victim of abuse responsible for the abuser's behavior. Victims become anxious when they have to be on guard all the time. They can never relax. They have to become mind readers or excellent interpreters of the tiniest hints given by the abuser's body language. They have to be able to read the abuser's mood instantly and correctly all the time. This constant tension is called "hypervigilance" and it is one characteristic often shown by people who've been through some traumatic or life-threatening experience such as being kidnapped, being a prisoner of war, or being beaten or raped.

> Brittany: *Jed was moody. When he was in a good mood, things were better. When he was in a bad mood, I'd either be quiet or*

try to do things for him to put him in a better mood. He'd criticize me for it. I was wrong no matter what I did.

LaShawnda: Terrell had a temper, all right. I thought I could be alert, see it coming. I even thought I could read his mind, know what was in his mind before he even did.

9. "Men are like that. That's just how they are."

Some victims may excuse abusive behavior by one boyfriend because they believe that all men are abusive. Perhaps their fathers and their friends' fathers were abusive, so abuse is all they know. But no one deserves to be abused, and no one is entitled to be abusive. There are many men and boys who have not grown up with abuse or who have chosen to lead nonabusive lives.

LaShawnda: I don't think I thought all men are abusive. But I liked my men tough. I'd dated some guys who were too nice. I thought they were wimps. I thought a real man shows his anger and doesn't take any crap. I didn't realize it was a recipe for abuse.

10. "If I can show him I love him enough, he'll stop."

This thinking error again makes the victim responsible for the abuse, when in reality, the abuser is the only person who can make it stop. This kind of thinking says that some shortcoming or lack of the victim's is the "cause" of the abuse. People who are being abused mistakenly believe that if their partners love them, they will not hurt them. Abusive behavior can occur whether or not an abusive person loves you.

Abusive behavior is most often an attempt to control the victim. And no matter how much you show that you love the abuser, he will not stop. The goal is control, not love.

> Juanita: I spent all my time trying to prove to Marco that I loved him and that I wasn't interested in anyone else. I thought I was doing something wrong that I couldn't convince him. He was so jealous, he accused me of having an affair with a guy I'd never even met. Sometimes he'd have me convinced I must be having affairs I didn't even know about — like multiple personalities — maybe a personality I didn't know about was the slut.

11. "I'm afraid he'll hurt me or my family if I leave."

Many times an abusive dating partner has made threats in order to keep someone in a relationship. He may have threatened to hurt the other person or someone in the person's family, such as a younger sister or brother, or even a pet.

> Juanita: Marco told me many times that he'd "let me have it" if I left him. He told me his cousin had a gun. He said he always knew where my mother was and where I was.

Being scared when threatened is not a thinking error, but letting fear keep you in an abusive relationship is. It's not going to get better — only worse. Report a dating partner who is making threats, even though the police can't do much. Get a restraining order or a protection order.

What Do You Think?

1. If you really wanted to be popular and have a boyfriend, would you put up with any of these guys? Why or why not?

2. How many of your friends think that they can handle everything in a dating relationship? Do you think that? Have you ever been in a relationship that you couldn't handle? What happened? How did you get out of the situation?

3. Karina and Brittany thought that they could get their boyfriends to change. Do you know anyone who has changed a boyfriend's behavior? What changed? How did she do it? Have you ever changed someone's behavior or attitude? What changed? How did you do it?

Things to Do

1. Have you used any of the 11 thinking errors described in this chapter? List the ones that you've used.

2. Using this list, try to brainstorm things you'd do differently or ways to counteract these thoughts so you won't get caught using the same thinking errors again.

Keeping a Journal

Write about how it would feel if you were in a relationship where you couldn't be yourself.

12 Breaking Through Your Denial

If one of my girlfriends told me that her boyfriend treated her like Marco treated me, I'd tell her he's a jerk and to drop him. But I couldn't see Marco's abuse because I loved him.

— Juanita

When you're in a relationship it can be difficult — but important — to recognize that you are in an abusive relationship and to believe that the abuse you are receiving is wrong. No matter what you do, no matter how sweet your dating partner is at other times, no matter how bad a day your dating partner has had, the bottom line is that you don't deserve to be abused.

So much denial — believing that nothing is wrong or trying not to see the negative, harmful parts of the relationship

— goes on that it may take months and sometimes years for a person being abused to break through her denial. But if you wait too long to admit that you are in an abusive relationship, you may be permanently injured or even die. If you are a victim of physical abuse, you need to realize that your relationship may be a time bomb ticking away, threatening your life.

To help break through your denial, keep a log or journal or diary of your dating partner's behaviors that match what you have read about so far. If there have been more than a couple of instances of emotional or verbal abuse in 12 months, you are probably in an abusive relationship. If there has been one incident of physical or sexual abuse in 12 months, you are probably in an abusive relationship.

> Brittany: *I found myself forgetting — denying? — the times Jed abused me verbally. If I'd kept some kind of journal or wrote in a diary, I think I might have left sooner.*
>
> Juanita: *I had never heard of emotional abuse. But if I had added up all the times I was unhappy, maybe I would have asked myself, "If I'm this unhappy all the time, why do I stay with Marco?"*
>
> LaShawnda: *When I'd hear about other girls getting beaten up by their boyfriends, I'd think, "What's wrong with them? I'd never let a guy do that to me!" But I let Terrell hit me. Maybe I would have seen how weak I was if I'd been writing about it all along. I mean, there would be proof, right in front of my face.*

Have any of your friends or family members shown concern about your dating partner's behavior? Are they shocked at how he treats you? If you have put off their concern by saying, "They just don't know him" or "They don't like him" or even "They're just jealous and trying to make trouble," those are thinking errors and should be a red flag. Your friends and your mom and dad are not going to like your boyfriend if they feel he mistreats you.

> Brittany: Some of my friends heard some names Jed called me. They asked me why I put up with it. I just thought, "They're jealous of me and maybe want to make trouble between us."

> LaShawnda: One of my friends tried to talk to me after I fell down the stairs — wait, I mean after Terrell pushed me down the stairs. She didn't believe that I'd just lost my balance — why should she when I'm all grace on the soccer field?

> Cathy: Nobody could say anything against Jerry because I didn't want anyone to know how bad things were. I was too embarrassed to admit he'd abused me. I thought my friends would think I was sort of stupid or pathetic. If they suspected about the abuse, they kept their mouths shut. Later, after I let him cut me off from my friends, I didn't have any friends left to tell.

Are you afraid of your dating partner? This should be a clue that he is abusive. Fear may be the one emotion that has escaped your denial that there is something wrong with your relationship. Listen to your fear — don't confuse it with excitement! Fear is built in to human beings in order to save our lives. Paying attention to your fear may save you a lot of hurtful time in an abusive relationship; it may even help save your life. Fear has no place in a healthy, loving, and safe relationship.

> Juanita: About two months into the relationship, I was afraid of Marco all the time. He had me so scared that I never dared think there was something wrong with him.

LaShawnda: I denied that I was afraid of Terrell. I kept telling myself that I could handle him. Even when he had a mean look on his face, I told myself that he was just angry, no big deal.

Cathy: I was in love. I kept saying to myself, you can't be afraid of someone you love. Wrong.

Have you changed what you say, how you act, how you dress, and how you spend your time in order to please a demanding and controlling partner? Do you feel forced to make these changes? Do you feel that you have to obtain your date's approval or change yourself to avoid being criticized? If so, your dating partner has you under control.

Here's another red flag: have friends or family said to you that you're not like yourself? Do they sense that you're not yourself even though they may not fully understand why?

Brittany: I changed from a pretty social, chatty, and easygoing person into a tense, quiet, more withdrawn person. I was always thinking ahead, planning what I was going to say to Jed so he wouldn't yell at me. Most of the time, he'd yell at me anyway.

Juanita: I had to get permission from Marco for almost everything. I tell friends now that if it had gone on much longer, I would have had to get his okay to go to the bathroom. He wanted me to check with him on what to wear if we were going out. How much makeup to put on. What food to cook. By the time it ended, I didn't feel like a real person anymore.

Cathy: I had changed so much that my mom and sister were telling me that I wasn't the same. They knew something was wrong, but they didn't know what to do. I didn't want to hear anything negative about Jerry from either of them.

Have you made excuses for your dating partner's behavior toward you? If so, you may be in denial.

> Juanita: I thought Marco did what he did because he cared for me. He told me a million times he loved me. I never realized his behavior was abusive.

> Cathy: Other kids would try to get through to me. No matter what they said, I came up with some excuse for Jerry's behavior. I'd never been that creative in my life. And all that time I spent covering up my bruises! One time my arm was bruised and my friend Ashley asked about it. I just told her I'd been wrestling with Joan's younger brother.

Are you more anxious than you were before you started dating this person? Being on edge is often a sign that you are in a difficult relationship.

> Juanita: I was tense all the time. Before I began dating Marco, I was having lots of fun. Things were looking up for me. I was starting to feel more confident about myself. Life with Marco was no fun, yet I stayed with him for so long.

> Karina: Every time Tyler came over, I tensed up. I was always worried that he'd pressure me to have sex, even when I wasn't interested. Come to think of it, I was tense all the time. Even when he wasn't around, I'd be worrying about the next time we'd be together.

Does your dating partner demand that you spend all your free time together? Have you given up your usual activities or interests to be with your dating partner all the time? Do you seem to have less of a life than you had before? Is your world smaller? Do you find that you're having less fun because your relationship partner is controlling what you can and can't do and how you spend your time? Do you feel like you're less of a person now? These are signs that you are in an emotionally abusive relationship.

> **Juanita:** *Marco was my shadow. Like a puppy dog. I had to be with him whenever I was free. He kept saying that's what people do when they're in love — they spend every minute they can together. I stopped all my other activities.*

Has your dating partner cut you off from your friends? Does he insist that you not see your friends or see only him or his friends? Does he criticize your friends? Is your partner extremely controlling, jealous, and possessive? This is a form of emotional abuse.

> **Juanita:** *Marco became angry whenever I even looked at a guy. He said we were flirting. He wouldn't let me include any friends when we were together. He didn't want me to see old friends, boys or girls. He put down guys in my cooking classes. It was like he had me locked up in some castle.*

Has your dating partner broken promises to you? Despite repeated promises not to yell at you or not to hit you, does your dating partner continue to abuse you?

> **Cathy:** *I'd be rich if I collected a nickel for every promise Jerry made. After a while, I'd ignore his promises. I knew they were meaningless. Yet I stayed with him, broken promises and all.*

Are you depressed? Crying a lot? Sleeping a lot? Having difficulty sleeping? Eating a lot more or a lot less than usual? Feeling sad all the time? Feeling helpless or hopeless? If you have become depressed or have developed signs of depression since beginning to date your boyfriend, you are probably in an abusive relationship.

> **Karina:** Only after I got out did I realize that I'd been depressed for ages.

> **Cathy:** I thought about suicide sometimes. I felt like there was nothing I could do to change the situation. Suicide seemed like the only way out of the mess. Besides, Jerry couldn't stop me. I took some pleasure in that thought — here was one thing I could do that he couldn't control! Fortunately, I came to my senses and realized that suicide was not the solution to my problems.

Has your personality changed since beginning to date your current partner? If your personality has changed for the worse, you may be in an abusive relationship.

> **Cathy:** I went from a happy-go-lucky kid to a very down and serious person. I had a chip on my shoulder.

> **Brittany:** I was pretty fun-loving before Jed. I became a loser. Nothing seemed fun anymore.

Has your dating partner talked you into doing things you never did before? Has he encouraged you to go against your values and beliefs? Are you now skipping classes, blowing off homework, smoking, drinking excessively, doing drugs, having sex, or breaking the law?

Dating should be fun. It should bring out the best in you, not pull you down. A dating partner who pressures you into doing things that aren't good for you is being controlling and emotionally abusive.

Karina: *Tyler pressured me into having sex before I was ready. Then he pressured me into smoking pot, telling me I'd enjoy sex more if I was relaxed.*

It is important that you face your denial honestly and squarely. Only by seeing your dating partner's behavior for what it is can you find the courage to get out of an abusive relationship.

What Do You Think?

1. Why do you think that the friends of these girls could sense that they were in abusive relationships but the girls themselves couldn't?

2. Why do some girls accept behavior from their boyfriends that they wouldn't tolerate from anyone else? Would you put up with otherwise unacceptable behavior from your dating partner? Where would you draw the line? What would you do if your dating partner crossed that line?

Things to Do

1. List the reasons why these five girls denied that they were in abusive relationships.

2. Read "That's All I Can Hope For" in *Dating Violence: Young Women in Danger* by Barrie Levy (check your town, county, or school library).

3. Go to a county or municipal court near you and ask to look at a restraining order (or protection order). Ask how much it costs to file one, how old you have to be, and how they are enforced.

4. Ask which judge hears most of the domestic violence cases. Sit in his or her courtroom and take notes. Do you see any similarities between these domestic violence cases and the experiences of the five girls?

Keeping a Journal

1. Write down some situations when you have felt afraid. How did you know you were afraid? Describe in writing the physical and emotional signs of fear.

2. Describe how it would feel if you experienced these signs every time you were with your boyfriend.

12
How to Leave the Relationship

Don't let your pride prevent you from telling someone. Tell the whole world if you have to!

—LaShawnda

Leaving an abusive relationship is not easy. It may be the hardest yet best thing you ever do for yourself. There are a number of steps to take once you decide to leave the relationship.

Speak Out

Tell several people — friends, family, a counselor or teacher you trust — that your relationship is abusive and you are leaving it. Speaking out helps break both the silence about dating abuse and the shame victims often feel. The shame belongs to the abuser, not the victim. Once people know the truth, they are more likely to support your efforts to leave. Also, they will want to know what's going on if it looks like you're going back to your abusive boyfriend.

Who can you tell? If you aren't totally cut off from friends, tell your best friend or all your friends. Some will be supportive; some might say, "I told you so." But others have to know before you can break loose. Believe it or not, parents can help, too. Once they calm down and get over their shock and anger, they can be supportive. You and your parents need to talk — and listen — and then you can work out how they can best help you leave the relationship.

A teacher or a counselor you trust or connect with at school can also support your efforts to leave a partner who is abusing you.

> Cathy: Once I told my mom, I knew I'd have the strength to leave. She kept me focused on what I needed to do. My sister helped, too. She talked to me. Made me promise to follow through.

> LaShawnda: I finally told a friend. She called me all the time to see how I was doing. She even made me go out to the movies with her because all of a sudden I had all this free time and nothing to do. It was good to get out of the house with somebody who was safe and believed in me — even if I couldn't really talk much with my jaw wired up.

Report the Abuse

If your boyfriend broke the law — if he assaulted or raped you or acted in other criminal ways — report him to the police. If your now ex-dating partner is stalking you, always appearing wherever you are or calling you on the phone or making threats, you may be able to report this behavior under some states' antistalking laws.

If you have reason to believe that your boyfriend will not stay away from you, consider getting a restraining order from a court. A restraining order (called a protection order in some states) is a legal document ordering someone to stay away from you. In some states, violating a restraining order is a felony, and the police can and will arrest the violator. But realistically, a restraining order is a piece of paper. It won't protect you from an abusive person who is determined to hurt you, without regard for the consequences. It can help, but it cannot guarantee your safety.

If there are later court proceedings, a restraining order provides evidence that you are serious about getting out of the relationship, that you've done everything you can to discourage contact, and that the other person is a threat. Many cities and counties provide advocates, usually from the victims' assistance office, who can support and advise you about restraining orders and sit with you during court proceedings. In some states, if you are under 18, an adult, perhaps a parent or a friend's parent, will have to help you get the restraining order.

LaShawnda: *I called the police and reported the assault. The police put him in jail. Steel bars between him and me helped me leave him. He couldn't hurt me anymore.*

Tell Your Dating Partner It's Over, Then Get Out

If you're having a hard time figuring out what to say and how to tell your abusive dating partner that you are leaving the relationship, practice with a friend. Try to role-play, with someone you trust pretending to be your dating partner (and if your friend knows the person you've been dating, so much the better). Ask for feedback about whether your message is clear. Practice as many times as necessary until you feel clear and strong in your message. Brainstorm with your friend some "what ifs" and how to deal with your partner's possible reactions in ways that keep you safe and get you out of the relationship. For example, "What if he promises he'll change?" You can remind yourself that abusers rarely change and almost never do so without help from a therapist, a special program for abusers, or an anger management program. Remind yourself of all the promises your dating partner has made and not kept in the past.

If you've been dating your abusive partner for a short time, he might accept it when you tell him that you don't want to date him anymore. When you tell your dating partner, be firm and clear. Don't confuse the other person by giving mixed messages about whether you want to get back together. Don't let your (ex-) partner think that some flattery and a little extra attention are all you want. Don't say maybe. Don't negotiate. Indicate that your decision is final. You don't have to shame or blame your dating partner; just be firm that the relationship is not working for you and that you're done with it. Tell him that you expect him to respect your decision.

If you've been dating your boyfriend for a long time or he becomes angry or violent quickly, you'll need to map out a plan for how to leave safely. In this situation, it might be safest to tell him by phone or in a public place with a safe way to get home. You may want to do it in the daytime when there are more people around. You may want someone with you, such as a close friend or parent. You may want someone else to tell him it's over, such as your older brother or your mother or father. Whatever it takes to give him the message clearly and keep you safe is okay.

> Brittany: I finally told Jed it was over between us on the phone. It helped me to feel safe.

Remember, your best chance for safety is to get out of an abusive relationship as soon as you see the first signs of abuse. That way, the abuser probably won't be as emotionally attached and will be able to let go more easily. Some girls who have stayed in abusive relationships for a long time have found that getting out safely is quite difficult. But even if the relationship has gone on for a long time, there is no excuse for abuse.

A few abusers never let go. They feel that if they can't have "their" girls, they don't want anyone else to, either. These abusers are dangerous and have been known to attack and even kill their dating partners when they tried to leave or get help. Some have killed themselves afterward. These men are filled with shame and are so insecure that they cannot face the idea that someone they thought was under their control would leave.

If you are scared of your boyfriend and fear for your safety, you can get a restraining order. If there is no safety at home, you can look up the number of a *safe house* for women or teens in the phone book. There are also victims' centers. When you arrive at the safe house or center, the staff will help you get out of the relationship safely.

Once you're out of the relationship safely, you may be able to return to school and go back to doing the things you used to do. In a few cases, a young woman may have to go to another school or move to another city and live with relatives because her dating partner is still a threat to her safety. Most important, once you get out of an abusive relationship, don't change your mind!

Spread the Word

It is a good thing to tell all your friends about your abusive (former) boyfriend. It's not enough that you're away from him — you don't want one of your friends to end up in a relationship with him. You don't want what happened to you to happen to your friends. But speak only about your own experience. It's not okay to say anything unless you know that it is absolutely true.

What Do You Think?

1. Do you think Karina should file a police complaint against Tyler for raping her? Why or why not?

2. Do you think Juanita should report being stalked by Marco?

3. How else could these girls let people know what they've been through or warn friends away from the boys they know are abusive?

Things to Do

Talk to your friends and find out whether any of them has ever left a relationship that was abusive. Ask them what they did to leave, who they talked to, and whether (and how) the other person tried to keep in touch with them. Ask whether they ever reported their dating partners' illegal behavior.

Keeping a Journal

Make a plan for how you would leave an abusive relationship and write it in your journal. Consider where you would tell your dating partner that it's over (a location that keeps you safe), who else in your life you would tell about leaving the relationship, whether you would report illegal behavior (and why or why not), and who you would go to for help if your partner wouldn't let go. If you're in a dating abuse support group, consider sharing your plan with others in the group.

13
Breaking Up Is Hard to Do

They just don't want to let you go. They call and call. They talk nice and sweet. You start asking yourself if you're doing the right thing. And you're so lonely at first.

— Brittany

Cathy, Juanita, Brittany, LaShawnda, and Karina attend a support group once a week. They have been successful leaving their abusive boyfriends. It wasn't easy.

Cathy: *Breaking up with Jerry was very hard. I cared for him. He cared for me. We had lots of good times, especially in between the bad times. Breaking up meant we weren't going to have any more good times. And since I didn't have any friends left, I felt like I'd never have any good times again ever.*

Brittany: I was frozen for the longest time. I wanted to get out but couldn't. I didn't know what to do. I'd been ground down to little pieces. I had no confidence in myself.

Cathy: Change was very scary for me. I was afraid of the emptiness in my life without Jerry. Who'd be my boyfriend now? Who would I go to the prom with? Who was I going to watch <u>Friends</u> reruns with?

Karina: Yeah, I felt that if I stayed away from Tyler, I'd never have a boyfriend again.

Juanita: I cried for weeks trying to decide what to do. For the longest time, I didn't even realize I was abused. I thought once I admitted that, it would be easy to leave him. It wasn't.

Cathy: I felt like I was making New Year's resolutions. I'd tell myself I was going to leave him, but I kept going back to him. I'd hold out and not see him for a few days and feel miserable. I had all this time and nothing to do but schoolwork, so I spent all that time mostly feeling miserable and thinking about Jerry.

Brittany: Jed didn't make it easy. He would never admit he was abusive. So I kept doubting myself. He kept calling and calling. I wanted to think this was all a dream — a nightmare, not really true. Then I could go back to him.

LaShawnda: I don't think I would have left Terrell if he hadn't hurt me so bad. Even so, I almost went back.

Cathy: One time Jerry sort of admitted that maybe his behavior was abusive. But he told me that it was my fault. Man, he never could take responsibility for his behavior.

Juanita: Marco always thought that I didn't listen to him enough. He blamed me for how he treated me. For a long time, I bought it.

Cathy: I think Jerry tried to get a grip for a while. He actually improved for a while, but then it was back to the way it was before. I kept thinking he should just be able to stop. I guess his abuse was sort of like a habit. It took me a long time to realize he wasn't going to change. At this point, my mom and sister talked to me a lot. I couldn't have stayed away from Jerry without their support.

LaShawnda: When I'd think about calling Terrell, I kept reminding myself that he almost killed me. If I had stayed in the relationship, he would have killed me. Even with him in jail, I'd think about him. Sometimes I felt sorry for him. And guilty for putting him there.

Brittany: When Jed was on his good behavior, I thought he wouldn't ever yell at me again. That was the hard part, remembering the sweet moments. Maybe, just maybe, it could be that way again.

LaShawnda: Terrell wrote me from jail. It was a very nice letter. I think he expects me to be at the door when he gets out. It'll be hard not to be.

Cathy: Jerry was such a large part of my life. I'd given up everything. I had nothing to do to fill my time. Lots of times I thought of calling him. To fill up time. I didn't know what to do with my free time anymore. I needed to get back into some activities and connect with some friends.

Brittany: Jed wrote me all sorts of notes, letters, poems. I'd get home from school and there would be flowers waiting for me. All the other girls were with their boyfriends. It was hard.

Juanita: I was used to being dependent on Marco. It would have been very easy to take him back. I was lonely most of the time. A couple of old friends realized I'd broken up with Marco. They called. They helped.

Brittany: They're so stuck on themselves that they think you'll never leave them. And then when you don't, they know they've got you. They know all your words are just empty threats. Jed's been telling the guys I'll break down and call him any day now. I hope I can resist. But then again, I guess that's why I'm here with you guys, so we can all help each other stay away from these control freaks.

Juanita: Even though I should be happy and celebrating, the truth is, I've never felt this sad. It's like a death in the family. You'd think my mom died.

LaShawnda: This Christmas was hard without him. It didn't feel like Christmas. Like Santa died.

Juanita: After I told Marco it was over, I'd get flowers and love notes begging me to reconsider. It was like there were two people inside of me. One wanted to take him back. The other didn't. I was fighting with myself.

Cathy: Once I told Jerry it was over, I was lucky. He didn't pursue me or threaten me. But even with all that abuse and what he said when I ended it, I still miss him. Sometimes I think I'm totally crazy.

LaShawnda: I knew Terrell wouldn't stay away. I reported him to the police and took out a restraining order against him. Once he was in jail, I felt safe. If he wasn't in jail, I might have taken him back at some point. Stupid.

Brittany: It's been about six months since I've been with Jed. It still hurts at times. I stare at the walls a lot. I think of how it might have been.

Cathy: I know I sound dumb, but sometimes I miss Jerry. I'd never go back to him, but there's still a part of me that loves him and cares about him. He just about destroyed me, but I still care for him. We had something special.

Karina: I'd ignored my friends for so long, I was too embarrassed to call them. They all seemed to have parties and things to do. Like they forgot about me. I don't blame them. That was hard. For a long time, I didn't have any friends to talk to, do things with.

Juanita: I was relieved when I got Marco out of my life. It's been months and I'm just now beginning to feel a little like my old self. When I go shopping for clothes, I still find myself wondering if Marco would approve. It's like I'm a trained seal or something. It's going to take a long time before I can do things and say things without wondering if Marco would say it was okay.

LaShawnda: Whenever I find myself doubting leaving Terrell, I remind myself that I'm lucky to be alive. I take out the pictures they took of me at the hospital and look at them. I wonder when I'm going to stop questioning myself.

Cathy: Breaking up is hard to do.

What Do You Think?

1. Which girl do you think is taking the breakup from her boyfriend the hardest?

2. Why do you think it's so hard to break up with an abusive boyfriend? If you were in an abusive dating relationship, what would make it hard for you to break up with your dating partner?

3. Even though Cathy feels very lucky that she was able to end the relationship without any threats or difficult behavior from Jerry, she still misses him. What are some reasons for missing him?

4. If you find yourself in an abusive dating relationship in the future, how easy or hard do you think it will be to break up the relationship?

Things to Do

1. If you have any friends who broke up with abusive dating partners, ask them how they felt the first week after the breakup. A month later. Now.

2. Ask them what they did to keep from going back to their abusive dating partners. Which things worked best?

3. If you are in an abusive relationship — or one that's becoming abusive — list steps you can take to get out of the relationship and stand up for yourself. Role-play with a friend some approaches to breaking up, and practice until you feel okay with doing it in real life. It may still be scary or make you nervous, but it's in your best interest to do it.

Keeping a Journal

1. If you ever broke up with a boyfriend, whether or not he was abusive, write about how you felt at first.

2. Write a letter to your "little sister," whose dating partner's abusive behavior has just put her in the hospital. What would you say to her? How could you be supportive?

14 Next Time

<u>Next</u> time? I don't want to even think about dating anyone. Ever.

— Karina

The girls continue to meet weekly. They talk about how difficult it's been to think about or have new boyfriends. They've lost their self-confidence. Some are distrustful of all boys now. They talk about what kind of dating relationships they want to have and what kind of personality and behavior they want in a new boyfriend.

Juanita: *I'm beginning to feel better about myself, but I'm scared about dating again. Right now, if any boy even looks like he's going to be nice to me or ask me out, I get nervous. I don't trust guys anymore. I'd probably end up in another abusive relationship.*

Karina: For now, I've sworn off guys, for like, maybe 20 years.

(All laugh.)

Cathy: I went out with a guy, and he did a couple of little things that reminded me of Jerry. I freaked. Didn't go out with him again.

Brittany: It'll be hard to feel safe with anyone.

Cathy: I don't think I'm going to feel comfortable being close with anyone for a long time. Jerry just about did me in.

LaShawnda: I've gone out with a couple of guys. I'm just not into it. One guy started talking loud because he was excited about the game we were watching, and it frightened me. Even though I know he's not Terrell, I kinda expected him to throw a punch.

Cathy: I know the signs of abuse now, but I still feel shaky and not very strong. I want a boyfriend so much that I might put up with some stuff. I mean, I hope I won't but . . .

Juanita: I have a lot of different expectations in mind now. I'd expect a boyfriend to treat me nicely. I hope if he starts treating me like Marco did, he's history. It's going to be hard because I worry that I'm all talk right now. I'm not sure that I'd be able to tell him to get out of my life. I'm afraid I might end up with another Marco. Have I really learned anything?

Brittany: Yeah, if a boyfriend ever raised his voice at me or criticized me, I hope I'd leave.

Karina: Tyler always pressured me for sex. I'd like to think I wouldn't keep going with someone who did that.

LaShawnda: *What I've learned is that when a guy gets angry real easily, watch out. You had that with Jed, too.*

Brittany: *Yeah, he'd get angry pretty quickly and start yelling at me.*

Cathy: *Jerry had an anger problem, also. I thought about leaving lots of times, but then he'd be as sweet as can be and I'd think, well, no, he really loves and cares for me. Why would I leave?*

Brittany: *That's the honeymoon period we heard so much about — when everything is peaches and cream until the next time he yells or whacks you one.*

LaShawnda: *We were all taken in by how quickly they can turn the sweet stuff on. And by how much we felt we loved them. And really, most of them don't get it that what they really want is control. They almost believe the stuff they tell us about how they'll never do it again, how much they love us. It's just that they don't do anything about how they take out their anger on the people around them.*

Juanita: *I need to recognize if anyone is ever playing mind games on me. Or if I'm not feeling like my normal self.*

Cathy: *Jerry consumed all my time. I was cut off from friends and family. I had stopped talking to my mom. Before Jerry, Mom and I talked all the time. Next time, if I feel a little weird about the guy I'm dating or when I feel bulldozed, I'd make sure I could still talk to my parents, or at least keep in close enough touch with my friends to talk to them about it. I won't let myself be so isolated again. I realize I let myself be a victim. I don't want to be a victim anymore.*

Juanita: Next time I date a guy more than a few times, I'm going to make sure I'm spending time with my friends, too. If he doesn't like my friends or doesn't want me to spend time with them, tough.

Cathy: I have to make sure I'm still doing the things I like to do. No guy is going to order me around, make me spend all my time with him. But if he's sweet, that's my downfall. I'd let him get away with a lot if he's sweet at least some of the time.

LaShawnda: Fear is what I have to watch for. Problem is, the littlest thing makes me afraid now.

Brittany: Any guy I date has to let me be myself and encourage me to do things that are good for me, not just good for him, or for his pleasure. I was a good student before Jed.

Karina: If I find myself unhappy around him, I need to end the relationship. Hope I can. I guess the lesson is that being lonely sometimes is better than being in a bad relationship, being unhappy and upset all the time.

Cathy: Any guy I date needs to treat me with respect. Encourage me to do my best in all areas whether or not it involves him. Encourage me to have friends.

LaShawnda: *We've all learned a lot — the hard way. The trick is to remember what we've learned and not allow ourselves to stay in an abusive relationship ever again. Some guy comes along and sweeps us off our feet and we're in love. Later, we find him being abusive or trying to control us. That's the test. If he flunks, get out. Stay out.*

What Do You Think?

1. Several of the girls think there is a possibility that their next boyfriends may also be abusive. Why do they think this? Do you agree?

2. Juanita says that her expectations of how a boyfriend should behave have changed. Next time, she'll compare how a boyfriend behaves with how Marco behaved. Do you think this is a good way to screen out abusive boyfriends? Why or why not?

3. LaShawnda and Brittany talk about the "honeymoon period" that sometimes follows abuse. Why would it be easy to be fooled by the "honeymoon period"? How can you tell whether to believe the promises your dating partner makes or whether your dating partner is sincere?

Things to Do

1. Make a list of how you expect a dating partner to treat you.

2. Ask some friends to make a list also. Compare lists.

3. Read *The Art of Loving* by Erich Fromm. Talk to your friends, teachers, and parents about it.

Keeping a Journal

Have you ever had experiences that made you feel less confident in yourself and your judgment? Write about them.

Lingering Effects

If I live to be eighty, I don't think I'll ever undo the damage Terrell did to me. Emotionally, physically, spiritually. I feel dead half the time.

—LaShawnda

The girls spend a few sessions together sharing how much damage has been done by their abusive boyfriends. They all feel beaten down emotionally, and some still mourn the loss of their relationships — or rather the loss of the *possibility* of a positive relationship. A couple of the girls are depressed and are getting counseling for their depression. LaShawnda wonders if she is ever going to look the same or be able to play soccer again.

> Juanita: I know I'll never be the same. I'll never forget what Marco did to me. And I don't want to forget.

Cathy: I think Jerry ruined it for me. I doubt I'll find anyone I clicked with like I did with Jerry.

LaShawnda: The romance is gone for me. It'll be hard for me to allow myself to love again. It's not just them. I don't trust me — or my judgment.

Brittany: I have no confidence in myself. There's still part of me that keeps thinking maybe I could have done something. Maybe it was my fault.

LaShawnda: There's a possibility, even with more surgery, that my jaw will never be right. And I have to get bone implants for my new teeth. I used to be nice looking. I'll never look the same again. The docs say I may have some permanent brain damage that will affect my coordination. I have headaches all the time. I may not play soccer again. I may not be able to go to college now. I was going to be the first in my family to go to college.

Juanita: I still have nightmares about Marco. And I'm nervous around guys. Last month I went out with a guy who said he liked the color of my dress. I almost slapped him. Another guy kept calling all the time. It felt like I was being abused again.

Cathy: I'm very angry at myself. Almost more angry at myself than at Jerry. I don't know how long it's going to take to stop being angry at myself. I feel so weak, like a wimp.

Juanita: I still find it hard to do things for myself. I was like a robot with Marco. I couldn't think for myself. I'm still having problems thinking and doing for myself. How long will it last?

Karina: It will be hard to have sex with another guy. Sex was so pressured that I don't think I'll be able to really know whether

I'm saying yes because I want to or because I'm afraid of what my partner will do if I try to say no. How can I enjoy having sex if I always feel like I'm being forced or tricked?

Brittany: If a guy is kinda nice, I'll always be thinking, okay, when is he going to start yelling.

Cathy: I'm still pretty depressed. My doctor says it might be a long time before I feel better.

Brittany: I'm still in a therapy group for depressed girls.

LaShawnda: Yeah, we've all been damaged. But we're alive.

Cathy: I cry all the time thinking about Paula.

Brittany: She didn't get out in time.

Karina: It could have been one of us.

LaShawnda: All the signs were there. She wouldn't listen to anyone — not that any of us was listening to anyone either.

Cathy: Her funeral was hard.

Eulogy for Paula

Cathy, Juanita, Brittany, Karina, and LaShawnda wrote this eulogy for Paula's funeral. LaShawnda read it at the service. Everyone cried. LaShawnda had to talk very slowly. Her jaw still hurt.

```
Paula was 17 when her boyfriend murdered
her. We all knew that Joseph beat her.
After a while, she didn't even bother to
```

cover up her injuries. We all knew. She knew we knew. Juanita and Brittany tried to talk to her. It seemed like she didn't want any help. She loved Joseph. She kept giving him second chances. She must have given him a hundred second chances. The next-to-the-last time he beat her, she was in the hospital for a month. I even visited her when my jaw was wired shut. Paula said she was going to leave Joseph. But we all knew she was afraid of him. Maybe she did tell him it was over. Over for her. Not for him. Joseph was going to show her. He went to her house, kicked down her door, and stabbed her 14 times. She was dead on arrival.

Before she dated Joseph, Paula was really cute. She had the prettiest long blond hair. She had a great sense of humor and lots of friends. Two years later, she was a mess. She tried to get out too late. Now she's dead, and Joseph is facing life in prison for killing her.

Did we fail her? I'll be asking that question for the rest of my life. Good-bye Paula. We love you.

What Do You Think?

1. Do you think all five girls will recover emotionally from their abusive relationships? What do you think it will take for each of them? How long do you think it will be before they feel able to date safely and confidently?

2. Karina worries that she may never be able to enjoy sex. Why could her bad experience with Tyler keep her from enjoying sex with someone else?

3. Several girls mention that they're almost as angry with themselves as with their abusive boyfriends. Do you think they'll get over their anger at themselves? Is that a good thing? Why do you think some of them are depressed?

Things to Do

1. Make a list of the harm done to each girl, according to what they've said.

2. What suggestions do you have for them to get over the damage that's been done to them? How can they move on in a healthy way?

3. Read "A Parent's Story" in *Dating Violence: Young Women in Danger* by Barrie Levy.

Keeping a Journal

1. Have you ever been depressed? Write about what triggers depression in you.

2. If you've ever been in an abusive relationship, write down the damage done to you.

16
Parents Talk: How Can We Help?

I wish there was a manual, like in the military. Something that told us what to do, what to say, and how to handle this situation.

—Karina's dad

The parents have their own support group. They're upset that their daughters were abused. They're angry that their girls kept the abuse secret. A couple of them wonder if they should have acted on their instincts that something was wrong. All of them wonder what they should have or could have done if their girls had told them that they were being abused.

Cathy's mom: I think Cathy didn't want anyone to know that Jerry wasn't the great, wonderful boy everyone thought he was.

She didn't want to admit that she couldn't handle the situation herself and was wrong about him.

Cathy's stepdad: She may have been afraid I'd go ballistic. Which I probably would have. I would have told her that she couldn't go out with him anymore. And that might not have helped.

Brittany's mom: Jed was always so nice and polite to me. He dressed nicely, held doors open. I never would have dreamed he was so foulmouthed. Even if Brittany had told me earlier, I might not have believed her. She may have sensed that and kept it hidden from me. I don't know.

Juanita's mom: Juanita would tell me a little about what was happening. But she only told me about Marco's jealousy. She seemed so pleased about all the attention he gave her. I never realized that he had her as controlled as he did. Juanita's father would have killed Marco if he'd known how Marco treated her.

Cathy's stepdad: Cathy was pretty secretive. If she had told us more, I probably would have had a problem with my temper. I might have called his parents. I don't know how Cathy would have taken it. We probably would have fought about it. How would that have helped?

Karina's dad: All those months Tyler was abusing Karina sexually, even raping her, she never let on. The thought still makes me want to beat that boy to a pulp! I think she was very ashamed, even though she had nothing to be ashamed about. She was tense and unhappy. We knew it had something to do with Tyler, but we didn't know what to do. I wish we had asked her if there was something wrong. Acted on our gut feelings.

LaShawnda's mom: LaShawnda's gone out with some pretty tough guys over the years. She was strong, though, and I didn't think anyone could do anything to her and get away with it. Terrell was special. She felt different about him. When he pushed her down the stairs, she made up some story that she just fell. The only one who knew what had really happened was her coach.

Cathy's mom: Cathy and I always did a lot of talking. This changed a few months after she started dating Jerry. I should have known earlier that something wasn't right. She seemed very depressed. I wish she would have asked for help from us. If not us, from someone. I wonder if she remembered the times her father hit me.

Brittany's dad: We didn't have a clue. Except that her grades began to slip. That was a big clue. She always did well in school.

Cathy's mom: Seems like most of our girls were pretty secretive. When we suspected something was wrong and tried to talk to Cathy, she just put us off. When I finally told her that she didn't look happy, I asked her if it had anything to do with Jerry. She broke down and cried and told me everything. Trouble is, she had been in this relationship for two years. Now she says she wished she had been more honest with us sooner. How do we get them to talk to us sooner?

Brittany's mom: It's hard to give help when you're not asked.

Karina's dad: But even if Karina had asked us, I'm not sure I would have known what to do, other than drag Tyler down to the police station. Karina would have resented me and defended him, probably would've gone back to him or stayed with him longer if I did that. If they think we'll go crazy, they won't tell us. We need to learn more about what to do and how to react if our daughters tell us they're being abused. If they tell us, maybe we should listen more and ask them what we can do to help.

LaShawnda's mom: LaShawnda's paying a big price for not telling anybody. She may not be able to go to college — we've been counting on a soccer scholarship to help. We don't know if she'll play soccer again. How do we get them to tell us what's happening?

Juanita's mom: There are a lot of things out there our girls think they can handle. The problem is, they can't. One thing we can do is to remember that they get in over their heads sometimes. We have to find a way so that they can talk to us. Tell us their worries.

Cathy's stepdad: Then we have to try to bumble along with them. Work together to try to help them figure out what to do. Listen more. If we come on too strong, they'll stop talking to us.

LaShawnda's mom: Then it's too late. They're laid up in the hospital, dead or unconscious, or with their jaw wired shut. Can't talk then.

What Do You Think?

1. What do you think these parents could have said or done that would have let their daughters tell them what was going on in their dating relationships?

2. What do you think these parents could have done to help their daughters get out of their abusive dating relationships sooner?

3. What would you say to these parents about how to encourage their daughters to tell them the first time their dating partners behave abusively?

4. How would you want your parents to react if you told them about an abusive dating relationship? What would be helpful?

Things to Do

1. Find out if there are any support groups for parents of teens in your town. Do any of them deal with dating or abuse?

2. Ask your friends if they've ever talked with their parents about their dating relationships. Make a list of the ways they started the conversations, where and when they were held, and whether your friends thought talking to their parents helped.

Keeping a Journal

Write about which of your parents you could talk to about an abusive dating relationship or another serious issue in your life. Why would you choose that parent? Where and when would you have the conversation? How would you start? How would you keep the conversation on track if your parent got upset?

How to Heal After an Abusive Relationship

There are several steps you can take to help yourself recover from the damage of an abusive relationship. These steps — many of them suggested by others who've been in abusive dating relationships — can help you get back your confidence and self-esteem and remind you that you don't have to let this experience keep you isolated as a victim.

- Keep a log or journal or diary. Try to write positive statements about yourself every day. List all the good feelings you've had since leaving your boyfriend.

- Reconnect with your old friends. Even though some of your old friends may be wary at first because you hurt their feelings when you dumped them in favor of your dating partner, at least some will be understanding and supportive and will welcome you back.

- Make new friends. Each new friend is a fresh start, without history or hurt feelings to come between you.

- Start talking to your mom or dad or another trusted adult (aunt, uncle, teacher, coach) again.

- Get involved with after-school activities to remind yourself that you can have fun and contribute ideas — and to occupy some of the time that you used to spend with your dating partner.

- Develop new interests, such as rollerblading or chess or singing or anything legal and positive that you can do with a few friends or a group.

- Learn to make decisions on your own again. Start with little decisions, every day: what to wear, what to eat, what to read, what to watch on TV, whether to do homework before or after supper. Then make bigger decisions: who to call or hang out with, what to do after school, whether to get a part-time job to earn spending money.

- Don't get involved with anyone who seems abusive in any way.

- Be a friend to others who are in abusive relationships — listen, be supportive, encourage them to get out, remind them that it's not their fault they're being abused and that they don't deserve it.

- See a counselor if you are very upset, unhappy, or depressed for more than a few days; unable to participate in your usual life and family activities; experience changes in eating or sleeping patterns; or begin using or increase your use of street or prescription drugs or alcohol.

- See a counselor if you have been involved in several abusive relationships. A counselor can help you figure out why you tend to pick partners who want to control you.

- Become a peer counselor at school so you can use your experience to help others. Being a peer counselor also lets you know that you're not the only one who has been through something painful. Helping others helps you remember what's good about yourself.

- Speak out about dating abuse. Let others know what it's like. Probably someone else will recognize her own situation in your story and not feel so alone and ashamed. She may see you as a role model — if you got out, so can she.

- Treat yourself well — you deserve it.

What Do You Think?

1. Do you think any of the steps in this list would help Cathy, Juanita, Brittany, Karina, or LaShawnda? From what you know about the girls, which of these steps might be more helpful to each specific girl?

2. How hard do you think it will be to actually follow these steps?

3. Would any of these steps help you? Which ones would you consider trying?

Things to Do

Make a list of volunteer opportunities and other activities a teenager could be involved in where you live or go to school. Check the phone book, ads looking for volunteers, church bulletins, and activities lists at school. Put a check mark beside the ones you might be interested in if you were coming out of an abusive relationship.

Keeping a Journal

Choose three steps that you think would be most helpful to you and describe how you would try them out, who you would have to talk to, and what activities you might choose.

18 Healthy Relationships

You may feel right now like you'll never want to date again or that you'll never find a dating partner who is not possessive, controlling, or abusive. But not all dating relationships are abusive. Many are healthy. What do they look like?

In a healthy relationship, both partners:

- respect each other and each other's feelings
- treat each other with thoughtfulness and consideration
- look for ways to have fun
- accept when the other person doesn't want to do something

- encourage each other to have friends and spend time with them
- support each other to do well in school or at work
- encourage each other to share or participate in making decisions
- believe that it's okay not to spend every minute with the other person
- try to support the other person to do his or her best
- find nonviolent ways to settle any conflicts

Healthy relationships *do not* involve:

- fear
- any kind of pressure, force, or violence (threats, shoving, slapping, hitting, arm-twisting, or other physical pain)
- disrespect
- unhealthy dependency
- possessiveness
- selfishness
- jealousy
- manipulation
- control

What Do You Think?

1. Think about your friends' experiences. What situations have they been in that showed features of a healthy relationship? Who were they with? What were they doing? What was the one thing that helped you see respect happening? How did you feel around them?

2. How can someone who has never felt respected learn to show respect for others and expect it for herself?

Things to Do

Ask your friends what "respect" means to them, and make a list. What behaviors show respect?

Keeping a Journal

Write about how you feel respected by your family, friends, teachers, or coworkers. Then write about someone in your life whom you respect and how you show that to him or her.

19 How to Be a Good Friend

Maybe your own dating partner is caring and respectful but you have a friend who is in an abusive relationship. You may wonder how you can help your friend, especially how to help her get out of that abusive relationship.

Here are some suggestions the girls in our group came up with:

1. Listen to your friend and believe her. Admitting the abuse to you is difficult for her. She is breaking away from her denial by telling about it, so help her continue by listening to her and supporting her.

2. Encourage your friend to find an adult to tell — a counselor or teacher at school, a good friend's mother, someone. She might have said that you are the only one she's told and sworn you to secrecy. Your promise of secrecy can get to be a heavy load, especially if she remains in the relationship or keeps going back to her abusive boyfriend.

3. Encourage her to leave the relationship.

4. If she doesn't identify her boyfriend's behavior as abusive but it is obvious to you that it is, explain to her that this behavior is abusive and that she deserves better.

5. Help your friend focus on her dating partner's abusive behavior, that her partner is responsible for his own behavior, and that she must get out before it gets worse. It doesn't help to give her pointers on how to stay in the relationship and not get hurt. That kind of advice only suggests that making the relationship work is totally her responsibility or that the abuse is somehow her fault.

6. If she tries to deny or minimize her partner's abusive behavior, challenge her denial. Remind her of her black eyes and bruises, the welts on her arms, how she's not the same person she used to be, and how completely controlled she is by her boyfriend. Label his behavior abusive. Don't let her call it something else. Let her know that she doesn't have to put on an act with you.

7. If she keeps going back to him, encourage her in a supportive (not critical) way to get some help. Anyone who can't keep away from an abusive relationship needs help in understanding how she is being manipulated.

8. Challenge it any time she says things like: "I deserve to be abused or hurt, I'm to blame for this abusive behavior,

I just keep doing things wrong, if only I kept my mouth shut," and so on. She's probably heard this from her dating partner enough times that she's accepted it as the truth. Tell her that no one deserves to be mistreated, ever!

9. Be prepared for the possibility that she may go back to him again and again, even after very abusive incidents. Remember, this situation is not about you — it's about her. Although it's frustrating, don't take it as a personal failure or as an insult from your friend when she goes back. You may feel repeatedly frustrated and even perplexed as to why she stays when it's obvious to you that the relationship is unsafe. Some girls make many attempts before they are finally ready to get away from and stay out of an abusive relationship. Remember: abusive partners are manipulators and masters of controlling everyone but themselves.

10. If you are concerned for her safety, tell an adult — her parents, your parents, a teacher, or school counselor. If you're worried that her dating partner is violent and that your friend might die (remember Paula), consider reporting the abusive boyfriend to the police. You may lose your friendship (she may be angry with you for telling the police), but you may save her life.

11. If you've been a supportive friend for a long time, and she keeps going back to her abusive boyfriend, you may have to tell her something like this: "I can't stand to be your friend and see you keep on being abused. It hurts me too much. I care about you a lot. I don't think I can continue to be your friend while watching you go back to him no matter how badly he hurts you." This step may lead you to withdraw from the relationship with your friend. It's not an easy step to take, especially if you're the

only friend she has left. But you may get to the point where you question whether you are doing your friend any good by just continuing to listen to her or watching her being abused month after month.

It's not always easy to be a good friend when someone you're close to stays in an abusive relationship and keeps getting hurt. Do your best to remain a friend, but remember, you have your limits, too.

What Do You Think?

1. Did anyone do any of the steps on the "how to be a friend" list for you? How did it feel? Did it help?
2. If you have done any of these steps with a friend, how did it go?

Things to Do

Ask your friends what help they would want from you if they were in abusive relationships. Take some time to consider what kind of help you would want from your friends in the same situation. If you or your friends have any ideas not already listed here, add them to the list.

Keeping a Journal

Write about your conversations with friends about their dating partners. Are any of them in a relationship like yours? If you were in a relationship that became controlling and abusive, how would you react if a friend tried to help?

20 Facts to Remember

1. According to a recent study by researchers at Harvard University, there is violence (sexual or physical) in one out of every five high school dating relationships. Other studies that include verbal and emotional abuse suggest that as many as one in three dating relationships involves abuse.

2. In relationships in which one partner shows low-level aggressive behavior (pushing, shoving, grabbing, pinning down), that partner often moves on to more severe levels of aggressive behavior (slapping, hitting, punching, choking, threatening to use or using a lethal weapon).

3. Dating aggression or abuse is most likely when the dating partners have become emotionally close. Dating aggression is less likely when partners have just begun to date or when there is no serious attachment.

4. When a male dating partner gets a girl or young woman pregnant, he is much more likely to abuse her.

5. Many girls and young women report that they behave aggressively as often as their male dates do. Girls and young women should take responsibility for their abusive behaviors. Abusive behavior is wrong, no matter who does it.

6. Girls often say that they are going to break up with their abusive dating partners. Often, they don't.

7. Some girls do nothing. Some girls tell other friends. A small number tell one or both of their parents, and an even smaller number report abusive behavior to a counselor or to the police.

8. Regardless of whether the abuse they experience is minor or serious, girls are just as likely to minimize it and pretend that it's not happening or that it was an accident.

9. Many girls accept some amount of violence and abuse in dating relationships. Until everybody rejects all types of dating abuse, it will be difficult to stop it.

10. Some studies suggest that as girls and women learn about abusive behaviors and their damaging effects, they become less willing to accept abuse in their lives.

11. Restraining orders are effective in many cases of dating violence. However, sometimes they are less effective when the abusers have been physically violent. These abusers often feel provoked by restraining orders and may violate them. This includes current and former boyfriends and husbands.

12. Studies show that verbal and emotional abuse can be just as damaging as physical or sexual abuse. Many people think that emotional abuse isn't serious, but it hurts just as much, and its emotional effects can last a very long time.

13. Some girls and women stay in their abusive relationships for many years. Some never get out. Studies suggest that the longer a woman remains in an abusive relationship, the harder it is for her to leave. The psychological damage is so severe that she feels completely helpless to do anything to get herself out. And often, she stays to protect her children.

14. Without counseling, girls who accept abuse as teenagers are more likely to accept abuse when they are adults. They go on to establish abusive relationships with future boyfriends and husbands. They either keep "choosing" or being attracted to abusive men or they never learn how to break the cycle and get out. They become victims of domestic violence.

15. Because some women who stay in abusive relationships have children, their children become victims of abuse. Between 50 and 60 percent of men who beat women also abuse children. (And without counseling, many of these children may grow up and abuse *their* children.)

16. When girls and women are in a committed relationship or are married with children, they often feel trapped — afraid to leave an abusive lover or husband. They may fear that they will be unable to support their families if they leave. Or their lovers or husbands have them controlled, isolated, and without friends.

17. Dating and domestic violence occurs every 15 seconds, every day. Make a point of reading your local newspaper or listening to the local news on TV. Read and hear about women who were in abusive relationships and how hard it was to get out. Some, like Paula, don't make it out. Some women and their children end up getting killed by their abusive boyfriends, husbands, ex-boyfriends, and ex-husbands.

18. Leaving abusive relationships before there are children is best. It makes leaving a little easier. It is a mistake to think that once the baby arrives he'll change.

19. Girls and women want to think that most rapists are strangers who leap out of dark alleys. This is not true. Most rapists know their victims at least slightly.

20. Some abusers abuse only when they are under the influence of alcohol or drugs. Alcohol and drugs have different effects on different people. They make some people short-tempered, belligerent, or violent. Drugs and alcohol may lower the inhibitions of other people enough to allow abusive behavior. If your boyfriend abuses only when he is under the influence of alcohol or drugs, he must obtain treatment in order for you to be safe. Very few people can stop their habits of drug or alcohol abuse without formal treatment (including going to a 12-step program such as Alcoholics Anonymous or Narcotics Anonymous).

21. Ten percent of girls and women report that they have been victims of date rape. Date rape is a very difficult crime to prosecute, since the rapist often says that the sex was consensual, that is, he claims that the girl or woman consented to having sex. A date rapist's defense lawyer will try to use the victim's behavior to show that she

invited or welcomed the sexual advances. Despite that, all victims of date rape should report it to the police. A boy or man who gets away with it once is more likely to do it again.

22. Almost all states have antistalking laws. If your boyfriend is stalking you, find out if your state has antistalking statutes. If so, report your boyfriend to the police.

23. Countless unwelcome telephone calls — with or without threats — are meant to control and intimidate. They are a kind of harassment that should be reported to the police.

24. Threats sent through the mail are also a form of harassment and should be reported to the postal inspector.

25. No matter what an abusive dating partner says or promises about changing his behavior, he will do it again. The best predictor of whether a person will be violent in the future is the *fact* that the person has been violent before.

26. Most abuse is hidden; it takes place behind closed doors. Both abuser and victim keep it a secret.

27. Fear is a survival signal. It shouldn't be ignored. If you are in an abusive relationship, it is important for you to listen to your fear. It may be the only part of you that isn't in denial. Listening to your fear can help you get out of an abusive and dangerous relationship. Listening to it and taking action to get out may be the difference between life and death.

28. A woman is beaten every 18 seconds in this country.

29. Recovering from the psychological damage of abuse is hard. Without help, some victims *never* fully recover.

Dating Abuse Summary

All abuse is wrong, no matter who initiates it — a boy or a girl. Violence during dating almost always continues into marriage.

A person shows acceptance of violence or abuse in a relationship when she:

- Stays in a relationship even when violence or abuse persists.
- Takes an abusive dating partner back time after time.
- Does not hold the partner accountable for his pattern of breaking promises repeatedly.
- Accepts responsibility for the partner's abusive behavior or emotions.
- Expects that the abuser will change or that she can change him.

- Makes excuses for abusive behavior or covers up signs of abuse.
- Denies to herself that her partner's behavior is abusive.
- Becomes violent or abusive herself.
- Keeps the abuse a secret.

Dating safely means:

- Identifying the abusive behavior.
- Refusing to tolerate or to accept excuses for abusive behavior.
- Getting out of an abusive relationship as soon as possible.
- Stopping your own provocative or abusive behavior.
- Telling a friend, a parent, a counselor, or the police about abusive behavior.

Remember, you don't deserve to be abused!

Glossary

Abuse To hurt someone by mistreating him or her; the behavior of mistreating by causing physical, mental, emotional, or sexual damage.

Coercion The use of emotional pressure, threat of harm, or physical force to get someone to do something he or she would not otherwise do.

Denial Pretending that a painful or difficult situation is not occurring; being unable to face a difficult reality. In this book, *denial* is used to describe the girls' reluctance to face the possibility that their dating relationships are abusive and unhealthy.

Emotional abuse A way of mistreating a person using such methods as isolation, control, jealousy, manipulation, threats, possessiveness, and unfounded criticism.

Fragile high self-esteem   High self-esteem (feeling very good about oneself) that can be easily threatened or lowered. When this happens, some people react angrily or aggressively.

Lethal   Something that can or does cause death, such as a severe head injury; a lethal weapon (such as a gun, car, or knife) can cause death.

Low self-esteem   The feeling that one is not a valued, cared-about, loved, worthwhile person.

Manipulation   A clever method of controlling a person — often using the person's own concerns or fears. For example, if a girl is afraid of her boyfriend leaving her, he may try to manipulate her into doing what he wants by threatening to break up. So, she does something she really doesn't want to do in order to keep her boyfriend. When manipulation is done successfully, the person being controlled often doesn't realize that he or she has been manipulated.

Obsession   A persistent idea, desire, or emotion that a person cannot get rid of. When one partner in a relationship will not let the other person leave the relationship, that partner is said to be "obsessed" with the person who wants to leave, or with being in control.

Physical abuse   A way of controlling a person by pushing, slapping, hitting, choking, shooting, stabbing, and so on; the causing of physical pain and harm to another person.

Provoke   To do or say something that annoys or angers another person.

Restraining order   A legal document obtained in court that orders one person to stay a specified distance away from and not to contact the person who got the order.

A violator may be arrested in some jurisdictions. Sometimes called a temporary restraining order (TRO) or a protection order.

Safe house   A place where abused and frightened people can stay for a short time while looking for a more permanent place to stay.

Self-esteem   To have good feelings about oneself. Pride and self-respect are part of self-esteem.

Sexual abuse   A way of controlling a person using sexual methods; using pressure, coercion, or force to make unwelcome sexual contact.

Shelter   A place a person can stay temporarily. There are often separate shelters for people who are homeless, abused, and so forth. Some large cities even have special shelters for teens.

Stalking   When one person pursues or follows another person or continues to make contact by phone, through friends, or in person with someone who does not want it. Stalking is done to intimidate, control, and, in some cases, harm the targeted person. **Cyberstalking** is unwanted contact or pursuit via computers and the Internet through chat rooms, e-mail, or instant messaging.

Verbal abuse   A way of controlling a person using verbal methods such as by yelling or using threats, put-downs, ridicule, and repeated and unwarranted criticism.

Appendices

APPENDIX A

How to Get Help

National

These organizations offer the names and numbers of local resources that can help you.

National Coalition Against Domestic Violence
1-800-799-SAFE

National Domestic Violence Hot Line
1-800-333-7233

National Mental Health Association
1-800-969-6642

National Organization for Victim Assistance
1-800-879-6682

National Victim Resource Center
1-800-627-6872

Infolink
1-800-FYI-CALL

Youth Crisis Hot Line
1-800-855-4663

Teen Hot Line
1-800-855-4673

Help against stalkers:

www.stalkingrescue.org

Local

Ask for help from the following:

> school counselor, social worker, nurse, or teacher
> peer counselor at school
> priest, pastor, rabbi, or other religious leader
> victim's assistance department at your local police department
> a best friend's mother or father

Consult the Yellow Pages of the phone book. Look under:

> Abuse Organizations
> Battered Women
> Crisis Intervention
> Domestic Violence
> Hot Lines and Help Lines
> Mental Health Agencies
> Rape Assistance Programs, Rape Crisis Hot Lines
> Safe Houses
> Shelters
> Support Groups
> Teen Organizations
> YMCA, YWCA
> Youth Organizations or Centers

Consult the White Pages of the phone book. Look up the agency if you know its name, or look in the Government Section for various agencies

Internet

Use popular search engines such *Yahoo!*, *Google*, *Lycos*, *Alta Vista*, and *Infoseek*. Suggested words or phrases to search for: dating abuse, teen dating abuse, dating violence, domestic violence.

Also, Infolink gives information about and referrals to victim assistance programs across the country. Web address:

www.nvc.org

APPENDIX B

Getting a Restraining Order

There are a number of steps to take if your dating partner has done any of the following: made threats to hurt or kill you; hit or pushed you; harassed you in any manner; or stalked you with repeated appearances, phone calls, answering machine messages, or e-mails.

If you've tried several things and your dating partner still won't get out of your life and leave you alone, you may need to get a restraining order, sometimes called a protection order or a civil protection order (see a sample restraining order on pages 142–43). Get a restraining order only if you are serious about ending the relationship and feel unsafe. Taking out a restraining order is a serious legal action, and you need to be sure that you don't want your dating partner in your life anymore.

Steps to Take

Call the courthouse beforehand to find out whether you need to be accompanied by an adult.

- Go to your county or municipal courthouse or offices.
- Tell the clerk that you want to fill out a restraining order.
- Be ready to pay a small filing fee, if required.

- In larger cities, there may be a victim's assistance staff that can help you fill out a restraining order. Find out the office hours and when you can meet with a staff member.

You do not need an attorney. Usually you are granted a temporary restraining order (TRO) right away; a few days later, there will be a short court hearing to obtain the permanent restraining order. This hearing is often before a judge or magistrate. Be sure that you know when it's scheduled and show up at the right time, and be prepared to wait if necessary (court schedules often change, and hearings may be delayed when other cases take longer than planned).

Once the temporary restraining order is approved, usually a law enforcement officer (sheriff or police officer) or a process server presents a copy to the person you have named in your restraining order. It isn't valid or in force until the named person receives a copy. The legal document orders the person named to stay away from you, often a certain distance away (200 feet, for example), and also not to contact you (such as by phone). The person named in the restraining order will also be told that any violation of the order carries the risk of arrest and imprisonment.

Obtaining a restraining order is a last resort, used when other efforts to keep your dating partner away from you have failed.

☐ Municipal Court ☐ County Court ☐ District Court
_____ County, Colorado
Court address:

Plaintiff(s)/Petitioner(s): _____
Address: _____

Defendant/Respondent: _____
Address: _____
_____

SAMPLE
Reproduction Prohibited

▲ Court Use Only ▲

Attorney or Party Without Attorney (Name and Address):

Case Number:

Phone Number: E-mail:
Fax Number: Atty. Reg. #:
The address of the protected party may be omitted from the written order of the Court, including the Register of Actions.

Division: Courtroom:

TEMPORARY CIVIL RESTRAINING ORDER
(This form is subject to the provisions of C.R.S. 13-14-101 to 13-14-102)

TO: _____, Defendant
Sex ☐ M ☐ F Race: ____ DOB: _____ Ht: ____ Wt: ____ Hair color: ____ Eye color: ____

The next hearing is _____ (date) _____ (time) at the court address above.
THE COURT FINDS that sufficient cause exists for the issuance of a civil restraining order.

You shall not injure, threaten, or molest the plaintiff or otherwise violate this order. A violation of a restraining order is a crime and may be prosecuted as a class 1 misdemeanor, municipal ordinance violation or a delinquent act (if committed by a juvenile) pursuant to CRS 18-6-803.5 and municipal ordinance.

1. *No Contact Provisions*
☐ It is ordered that you, the defendant, **shall have no contact of any kind** with the plaintiff(s), with the following exceptions:
_____

☐ You must keep a distance of at least _____ yards from the Plaintiff(s).

2. *Exclusion from places*
It is ordered that you are excluded from the following places: (Please specify address)
☐ Home: _____
☐ Work: _____
☐ School: _____
☐ Other: _____
_____

☐ Exceptions: _____

You may not remain in or return to any of the above locations after you receive this order. You shall be permitted to return to a shared residence one time to obtain sufficient undisputed personal effects necessary to maintain a normal standard of living ONLY if you are accompanied at all times by a peace officer.

3. *Care and Control Provisions*
☐ It is in the best interest of the minor child(ren) named below that care and control of these child(ren) be awarded to:
_____ until the next hearing. At that time, the court will determine who should receive temporary care and control of the minor children for up to 120 days.
Name: _____ DOB: _____
Name: _____ DOB: _____
Name: _____ DOB: _____
Name: _____ DOB: _____

A PEACE OFFICER SHALL USE REASONABLE MEANS TO EFFECTUATE THIS CARE & CONTROL ORDER.
JDF 398 R11/99 TEMPORARY CIVIL RESTRAINING ORDER (Page 1)

(1) Court Copy   (2) Plaintiff Copy   (3) Distribute as Applicable   (4) Distribute as Applicable

4. **Issues Concerning Children**
☐ Parenting time (visitation) will be considered at the permanent orders hearing.
☐ Parenting time (visitation) shall be as previously ordered by the _____ District Court. Case #_____
☐ You shall have no contact with the following minor children:
Name: _____ DOB: _____
Name: _____ DOB: _____
Name: _____ DOB: _____
Name: _____ DOB: _____

5. **Other Provisions**
☐ It is further ordered that:_____
_____
_____
_____
_____

SAMPLE
Reproduction Prohibited

_____   _____   _____
Judge/Magistrate   Date   Print Judge/Magistrate name

WARNING: A violation of a restraining order may be a class 1 misdemeanor, municipal ordinance violation or a delinquent act (if committed by a juvenile). Anyone over the age of eighteen who violates this order may be subject to fines of up to $5000 and up to 18 months in jail. Violation of this order will constitute contempt of court. A juvenile adjudicated may be subject to commitment to the Department of Human Services for up to two years. **You may be arrested or taken into custody** without notice if a law enforcement officer has probable cause to believe that you have violated this order. If you violate this order thinking that the other party or anyone else has given you permission, **you are wrong**, and can be arrested and prosecuted. The terms of this order cannot be changed by agreement of the parties. Only the court can change this order.

NOTICE TO DEFENDANT: YOU ARE DIRECTED TO APPEAR BEFORE THIS COURT ON THE DATE SHOWN ON THE FRONT OF THIS FORM TO SHOW CAUSE, IF ANY EXISTS, WHY THIS TEMPORARY RESTRAINING ORDER SHOULD NOT BE MADE PERMANENT. YOU ARE FURTHER ADVISED THAT IF YOU FAIL TO APPEAR AT COURT IN ACCORDANCE WITH THE TERMS OF THIS ORDER, A WARRANT MAY BE ISSUED FOR YOUR ARREST. IF THIS ORDER IS TO PREVENT DOMESTIC ABUSE, THIS TEMPORARY RESTRAINING ORDER SHALL BE MADE PERMANENT WITHOUT FURTHER NOTICE OR SERVICE. YOU ARE NOTIFIED THAT THE PERMANENT RESTRAINING ORDER SHALL REMAIN IN EFFECT UNTIL FURTHER ORDER OF THE COURT. SUCH PERMANENT ORDER WILL SUBJECT YOU TO FEDERAL LAW RESTRICTING FIREARMS POSSESSION AND SALE [18 U.S.C.A. 922(g)].

NOTICE TO PLAINTIFF: YOU ARE HEREBY INFORMED THAT IF THIS ORDER IS VIOLATED YOU MAY CALL THE POLICE, INITIATE CONTEMPT PROCEEDINGS AGAINST THE RESTRAINED PERSON IF THE ORDER IS ISSUED IN A CIVIL ACTION OR REQUEST THE PROSECUTING ATTORNEY TO INITIATE CONTEMPT PROCEEDINGS IF THE ORDER IS ISSUED IN A CRIMINAL ACTION.

NOTICE TO PEACE OFFICERS: You shall use every reasonable means to enforce this restraining order. You shall arrest or take into custody, or if an arrest would be impractical under the circumstances, seek a warrant for the arrest of the restrained person when you have information amounting to probable cause that the restrained person has violated or attempted to violate **any provision of this order subject to criminal sanctions pursuant to CRS 18-6-803.5 or municipal ordinance** and the restrained person has been properly served with a copy of the restraining order or the restrained person has received actual notice of the existence and substance of such order. You shall enforce this order even if there is no record of it in the Restraining Order Central Registry. You shall take the restrained person to the nearest jail or detention facility. You are authorized to use every reasonable effort to protect the alleged victim and the alleged victim's children to prevent further violence. You may transport, or arrange transportation to a shelter for the alleged victim and/or the alleged victim's children.

JDF 398   R11/99   TEMPORARY CIVIL RESTRAINING ORDER   (Page 2)

(1) Court Copy   (2) Plaintiff Copy   (3) Distribute as Applicable   (4) Distribute as Applicable

APPENDIX C

Sexual Abuse

Many girls and women are not sure exactly what sexual abuse is. They are confused by what they hear from friends or see on TV or in the movies. Their boyfriends add to this confusion with statements like "You came on to me" or "You said you wanted to" or "You were enjoying it."

Any sexual behavior that is forced on you is sexual abuse. "Force" can include emotional and verbal strategies that are manipulative and controlling. Karina's boyfriend Tyler used many common emotional and verbal strategies, including:

- Telling Karina that she should "prove" her love by having sex with him.

- Threatening to leave her if she didn't have sex with him.

- Putting her down by implying that she must be frigid.

- Not listening to her when she said she wasn't emotionally ready.

- Discounting her concerns about getting pregnant or catching a sexually transmitted disease.

Eventually, he also physically forced her to have sex — he raped her.

Sexual abuse is not just intercourse, or penises in vaginas or anuses or mouths. It can involve any sexual behavior, including unwelcome touching, coercing a person to dress in a sexually provocative manner, pressuring a person to talk in a sexual way, pressuring a person to look at pornographic magazines or videos, and so on.

Any time you say no or express disinterest in engaging in any type of sexual behavior, a loving partner listens to you and honors your feelings and doesn't continue to push for sex. When a dating partner does otherwise, what's going on is sexually abusive.

Sexual abuse, like all the other kinds of abuse, is controlling and manipulative. Don't let yourself be controlled or manipulated into any type of unwanted sexual behavior.

APPENDIX D

Date Rape Drugs

By now, it's almost old news: beginning in the 1980s and 1990s, some would-be rapists figured out that their illegal sexual activities would be easier if they drugged their intended victims. They used one of the two or three "new" drugs administered by dropping them into girls' drinks. These drugs are prescription sedatives usually used by people with insomnia, by people going into surgery, or by those working on therapy issues under hypnosis. Most are not legal and are not prescribed in the United States, but they're smuggled in from other countries and often sold singly by the pill.

Rohypnol (also known as roofies, roaches, and ruffies, among other names) is one of the better-known drugs. The generic name is flunitrazepam (floon-y-TRAZ-eh-pam). It dissolves quickly and doesn't have much taste, so it is hard to detect. In combination with alcohol, it makes you feel much drunker than you would be after just one drink. It makes you pass out, and when you wake up, you don't remember anything that happened. That's how a date rapist wants it — no memories about how he took advantage of you while you couldn't give legal consent.

Another drug in the same family is legal in the United States. Klonopin (KLON-oh-pin), the brand name for clonazepam (clo-NAZ-eh-pam), is a prescription drug that's used to calm people down when they're anxious and upset. It has similar effects as Rohypnol when used with alcohol and is sometimes sold as roofies on the street.

GHB is gamma hydroxybutyrate (GAM-ma hy-DROX-y-bu-TY-rate), another date rape drug. It can cause you to pass out, forget what happened, or even have seizures. It also can cause you to throw up and have problems breathing.

Ketamine (KET-ah-meen), the third major date rape drug, is also known as special K, vitamin K, and Kat, among other names. It is used by veterinarians to tranquilize sick or injured animals. It separates your consciousness from your body — you're awake, sort of, but you don't seem to care about or have any control over what you're doing. It blocks any input from your senses to your brain — so for instance, someone could punch you, and you wouldn't feel it at the time, but you might come out of it with a bad bruise or even a broken bone. Date rapists like this drug because their victims don't struggle, since they don't feel any pain from the unwanted sexual contact. According to some sources, this drug can affect your judgment and coordination for up to 24 hours.

How does this happen? A girl or woman might be at a party, and when she's not looking, her date slips one of the date rape drugs into whatever she's drinking. The sedating effects usually begin within minutes of drinking the drugged beverage.

Bottom line: don't leave any drink unattended, whether it's soda or beer or a mixed drink. Get your own refills. Watch the bottle being opened. Watch out for friends at parties, and ask them to watch out for you.

If you see someone acting a lot drunker than she should be for the amount of alcohol consumed, get that person to an emergency room fast! Tell the nurses or doctors that your friend needs to be tested for a date rape drug. If they need more information on the testing, they can call 1-800-608-6540, which connects them to the company that makes Rohypnol.

If you feel weird after a drink or two, ask a trusted friend to drive you to an emergency room or to call 911 immediately!

If you wake up with no memory after a party or a date, there's a chance that you were drugged and sexually assaulted. Call a rape hot line and ask someone to take you to the hospital or meet you there. Don't shower or change clothes, but take a spare set of clothes to change into later. Ask to be tested for a date rape drug, and ask to have a "rape kit" or sexual assault examination done. This is all very hard to deal with, but it's the only way that rapists get caught.

Nothing you did while under the influence of a date rape drug is your fault. Even if you "consented" to intercourse, if you have been given a date rape drug, the law states that this is rape. Legally, a person under the influence of alcohol or drugs cannot give sexual consent.

And remember, even though they are called *date* rape drugs, the fact is that anyone can put a drug into your drink when no one is looking, then follow or escort you out of the room and do whatever he wants after you pass out. Although rapists are often known to their victims, a rapist who slips a date rape drug into a woman's drink may not be her date and may even be a complete stranger.

APPENDIX E

Are You Depressed?

No one should diagnose herself for depression or any other major emotional problem. For many reasons, it can be difficult to separate a temporary depression from something long term that requires professional help. Given that caution, read some of the signs of depression below and ask yourself if they apply to you. Even if a number of them do, this does not mean that you are depressed in the clinical sense, but you should try to find a counselor or doctor who is trained in diagnosing depression in teenagers to find out what's really going on. Depression is easily treatable with professional help.

Signs of Depression

1. You feel sad or empty for more than two weeks.

2. You feel tired most of the time.

3. You feel hopeless, guilty, or worthless for several weeks.

4. You have trouble sleeping, or you sleep too much.

5. You find it difficult to make decisions, or you have a hard time concentrating.

6. You are bored a lot with yourself, others, and life in general.

7. You either eat all the time or have little or no interest in food.

8. You are withdrawing from others.

9. You are acting out or getting in trouble at school.

10. You are getting in trouble with the law.

11. You don't feel well. You have lots of headaches, stomachaches, or other physical symptoms.

12. You're not the same person you were. Your personality has changed. Friends or family members have told you that you seem different. You used to be happy and confident, but now you are depressed, fearful, or angry. Or you used to be a gentle person, but now you are aggressive.

If you've answered yes to a number of these statements, there is a possibility that you are depressed. Go to your school nurse or counselor and ask for help.

APPENDIX F

When a Girl Is the Abuser

As mentioned earlier in this book, sometimes girls are the abusers, either in a relationship with a boy or in a same-sex relationship with another girl. This situation is more common than most people think. In some cases, the girls are retaliating, fighting back in order to defend themselves against abusive boyfriends.

If girls find themselves being abusive, they should definitely get out of the relationship and get help to change their behavior. Even when the abuse is self-defense, the odds are high that girls in such mutually abusive relationships are going to get hurt.

Some girls initiate the abuse in a dating relationship. They use verbal abuse (all forms), emotional abuse (especially possessiveness and jealousy), and physical abuse (mainly slapping, hitting, pulling hair). Just as any kind of abuse is unacceptable for males, it is equally unacceptable for females, regardless of the gender of their dating partners.

It is a rare dating partner who will report or try to stop his girlfriend's abuse. Most boys are afraid of being seen as wimps if their friends find out. They're afraid of being laughed at by both male and female peers.

Many boyfriends just blow off their girlfriends' abuse. Some of them think it's "funny." They usually don't take physical abuse seriously because they aren't afraid. Most boys feel that they can't be seriously hurt by a smaller, and usually weaker, girlfriend.

Even if your boyfriend seems to tolerate your abuse, you need to get out of this relationship and get some help. First, it's unhealthy to be abusive. You won't be proud of it later in life, and it'll be a lot harder to stop if it becomes a long-term habit. Second, someday you're going to hit the wrong guy — a guy who is twice your size, has a temper, and doesn't like being hit. If you hit this guy, he may become so enraged that you end up in the hospital or, like Paula, dead. Don't live your life in this danger zone.

APPENDIX G

Questions and Answers

Q. How can I leave him? He loves me.

A. It may be true that your boyfriend says he loves you. However, what kind of love is it when he shows his love by abusing you? Perhaps he puts you down all the time or threatens you or hits you. This is not a love that is caring or nurturing. It is not a mature or healthy love. You can end up very badly injured or dead with this type of love. Is this the kind of love you really want? Or really deserve?

Q. Why can't I just stay with him and help him change?

A. No boyfriend will change unless he wants to change. You can't make him change. He can change only if he admits that his behavior is abusive, gets professional help, and makes a total commitment to stop it. Only with professional help can he begin to understand that his abusive behavior is about his need to control, dominate, and humiliate. This is a therapeutic issue that takes skill and experience to deal with. You do not have the training necessary to help your boyfriend. And as long as you stay with him, there's no reason for him to change. What he's doing to you has worked to get him what he wants so far.

Q. I know he wants to change. He keeps making promises, but he can't keep them. Why?

A. Your boyfriend's need to control and dominate is a deep need for him. His controlling behavior has also become a habit. Deep needs and habits do not change quickly, and they do not change without some professional help.

Q. If I tell my parents, they'll just order me not to see him anymore. What do I do?

A. Most parents will not be happy to learn that their daughter's boyfriend has been abusing her. They may get really angry at your boyfriend or even at you. Remind them that what you need right now is their love and support. Many parents will not be completely shocked — they may have suspected that something wasn't quite right with your relationship. If you want to break up with your boyfriend, telling your parent or parents is a good thing. First, your secret is out. Abuse should not be a secret. Second, if your parents do say that you shouldn't see him anymore, you can tell your boyfriend that. Your parents will probably be happy to take the blame for your breakup. Once he knows the secret is out — that your parents know about his abusive behavior — he may stay away.

Q. What if I'm okay with his jealous and possessive behavior?

A. Many girls and women believe that emotional (and verbal) abuse is less serious than physical or sexual abuse. This isn't true. Therapists who work with girls and women who have been abused find that the effects of emotional and verbal abuse can be just as damaging as the effects of physical and sexual abuse. Girls and women also tend to believe that the abuse won't get any worse. By the time it does get worse — and it will — they may not have the strength it takes to leave the relationship. It's not much of a stretch for a boyfriend to go from being emotionally abusive to being physically or sexually abusive, since the underlying need of all dating abuse is the same: the need to control, dominate, and humiliate.

Q. I was doing okay for a while after I broke up with my boyfriend, but I still miss him. What do I do?

A. Keep reminding yourself of his abuse. Picture it clearly in your mind. Tell yourself that this is why you broke up with him in the first place. It is important to do this, because memory can play tricks on a person. Over time, a person's memory of abuse often weakens. Or it may become so hazy that you question whether the abuse ever took place. Also, make sure that you're connecting with friends and activities that you enjoy. Do special things for yourself. Eventually, you will be able to say, "I miss him, but I don't miss his abuse." This is okay. You're making progress. Don't expect to get over him quickly.

Q. My boyfriend has been physically abusive. Should I report him to the police?

A. Yes. Many boyfriends don't realize that their abusive behavior is criminal — it's against the law. If you report his abuse to the police, your boyfriend will learn that his behavior is criminal, and he may be charged. If convicted, he may have to serve some time in jail, be fined, or be put on probation. He'll also learn that this is not an okay way to behave toward women.

Q. Isn't some of this my fault? After all, I let the abuse go on for so long.

A. Ask yourself this question *after* you get out of your abusive relationship. You can take some responsibility for allowing yourself to stay in an abusive relationship, but don't be too hard on yourself. Perhaps some of the delay was understandable:

- It took you a while to realize that your boyfriend's behavior was abusive.
- You believed your boyfriend when he promised that he would change — he was very convincing.
- You thought you had done something to cause his abuse.
- You thought you understood it, so you thought you could "control" it by doing or not doing certain things (dressing a certain way, not talking to other boys, ignoring your friends).
- He had you scared about leaving the relationship.

But you are not responsible for the abuse itself. No one deserves to be abused, and you certainly didn't. Instead of blaming yourself too much, give yourself lots of credit for getting out.

Q. What are the chances that my next boyfriend will be abusive?

A. Unless you learn from experience and make sure that you get going before the going gets rough, your chances of being in another abusive relationship are very high. You should think about the relationship you just got out of and try to understand it. Were there signals that you missed? Were there signs that you minimized or denied? Were you so desperate for a boyfriend that you put up with his abuse? Was your self-esteem so low that you didn't think a popular, healthy boy would be interested in you? If you can understand your vulnerabilities, you can be more cautious in the future. Then, hopefully, you will be alert to any signs of abuse early on in a new relationship. If there are such signs, you need to make a commitment to yourself to end the relationship immediately.

Q. **What's the first thing I should do when I get out of an abusive relationship?**

A. *Celebrate!* Enjoy your freedom. Cheer yourself for caring about your physical safety. But also give yourself permission to feel sad and mourn the loss of the relationship, even though it got so bad. Most people coming out of a long relationship feel sad that it didn't work out and that the possibility of having something great with that person is gone because of abuse. Take pleasure in making your own decisions. Feel good about doing what you want. Relish being in control of your life. Do some things that your boyfriend wouldn't let you do. Connect with friends he cut you off from. Wear clothes you like. Go places he didn't want to go to. Promise yourself "never again."

APPENDIX H

Further Reading

Periodicals

Journals, magazines, and newspaper articles can be located and often accessed on the Internet or in your public library. Check the *Reader's Guide to Periodical Literature* under "date rape" or "dating violence." A few helpful magazine articles are the following:

"Boy Meets Girl, Boy Beats Girl," by Michele Ingrassia. *Newsweek*, December 13, 1993.

"Date Rape: The Scary Truth," by Joseph Weinberg. *Teen Magazine*, April 1995.

"Mad Love," by Sabrina Solin. *Seventeen*, March 1996.

"What You Need to Know" (coping with potentially violent boyfriends), by Christopher Carstens. *Teen Magazine*, June 1996.

Books

These books are available through your town or school library or through interlibrary loan. Check your library's listings, either on computer or in a card catalog, under "dating abuse," and you may find other titles.

Dating Violence: Young Women in Danger
   by Barrie Levy

Date Abuse
   by Herma Silverstein

Everything You Need to Know About Abusive Relationships
   by Nancy Rue

The Gift of Fear
   by Gavin de Becker

Staying Safe on Dates
   by Donna Chaiet

Update: Date Rape
   by Alexandra Bandon

The Battered Woman
   by Lenore Walker

Next Time She'll Be Dead
   by Ann Jones

About the Author

Nicole B. Sperekas, Ph.D., is a psychologist who helps children and adolescents. She is also the author of *SuicideWise: Taking Steps Against Teen Suicide* (Enslow Publishers, 2000).

Dr. Sperekas began working with abused children and adolescents when she directed a program for people who had been sexually assaulted. Some of the teenagers she treated told her of their experiences with dating abuse. Dr. Sperekas has seen the number of reported cases of dating abuse increase dramatically over the years. She hopes that this book will alert teens to the frequency and seriousness of this problem. Dr. Sperekas's work is based on two strong beliefs: abusive boys and men have to learn that abuse is not acceptable and change their behavior, and girls and women must learn not to tolerate abusive behavior from their dating partners.

About Safer Society Press

The Safer Society Press is part of The Safer Society Foundation, Inc., a 501(c)3 nonprofit agency dedicated to the prevention and treatment of sexual abuse. We publish additional books, audiocasettes, and training videos related to the treatment of sexual abuse. To receive a catalog of our complete listings, please check the box on the order form at the back of the book and mail it to the address listed or call us at (802)247-3132. For more information on the Safer Society Foundation, Inc., visit our website at www.safersociety.org.

Selected Safer Society Publications

Outside Looking In: When Someone You Love is in Therapy by Patrice Moulton and Lin Harper (1999). $20.

When You Don't Know Who to Call: A Consumer's Guide to Selecting Mental Health Care by Nancy Schaufele and Donna B. Kennedy (1998). $15.

Shining Through: Pulling It Together After Sexual Abuse by Mindy Loiselle and Leslie Bailey Wright (1997). $14. For girls ages 10 and up.

Back on Track: Boys Dealing with Sexual Abuse by Leslie Bailey Wright and Mindy Loiselle (1997). $14. For boys ages 10 and up.

From Trauma to Understanding: A Guide for Parents of Children with Sexual Behavior Problems by William D. Pithers, Alison S. Gray, Carolyn Cunningham, and Sandy Lane (1993). $5.

Roadmaps to Recovery: A Guided Workbook for Young People in Treatment by Timothy Kahn (1999). $20. For children ages 8 and up.

Tell It Like It Is: A Resource Guide for Youth in Treatment by Alice Tallmadge with Galyn Forster (1998). $15. Testimony from teens who have been in treatment for sexual offending.

Healthy Thinking/Feeling/Doing from the Inside Out: A Middle School Curriculum for the Prevention of Violence, Abuse & Other Problem Behaviors by Jack Pransky and Lori Carpenos (2000). $28.

When Your Wife Says No: Forced Sex in Marriage by Fay Honey Knopp (1994). $7.

Man-To-Man, When Your Partner Says NO: Pressured Sex and Date Rape by Scott Allen Johnson (1992). $8.

SOS Help for Emotions: Managing Anxiety, Anger, and Depression by Lynn Clark, Ph.D. (1998). $13.50 Parents Press.

ORDER FORM

Date:_____

All books shipped via United Parcel Service. Please include a street location for shipping as we cannot ship to a Post Office address.

SHIPPING ADDRESS:

Name and/or Agency _____

Street Address (no PO boxes) _____

City _____ State _____ Zip_____

BILLING ADDRESS (if different from shipping address):

Address _____

City _____ State _____ Zip_____

Daytime phone (____)_____ P.O.#_____
                                                             (must be submitted)

Visa or MasterCard # _____ Exp. Date _____

Signature (for credit card order)_____

☐ Please send me a catalog.   ☐ Do not add me to your mailing list.

QTY	TITLE	UNIT PRICE	TOTAL COST
		SUBTOTAL	
		VT RESIDENTS ADD 5% SALES TAX	
		SHIPPING (SEE BELOW)	
		TOTAL	

No returns.
All prices subject to change without notice.

Bulk discounts available, please inquire.
All orders must be prepaid.

Phone orders accepted with MasterCard or Visa.
Call (802)247-3132 or fax (802)247-4233.

Make checks payable to: **SAFER SOCIETY PRESS**

www.safersociety.org

Mail to:

Safer Society Press
PO BOX 340 • BRANDON • VT 05733

A program of The Safer Society Foundation, Inc.

Shipping and Handling

1–4 items	$5	21–25 items	$17
5–10 items	$8	26–30 items	$20
11–15 items	$12	31–35 items	$23
16–20 items	$14	36–40 items	$26
	41–50 items	$31	
	51+ items	call for quote	